GREAT JOBS

JOBS

FOR

Foreign Language Majors

Third Edition

GREAT JOBS

FOR

Foreign Language Majors

Julie DeGalan and Stephen Lambert

New York Chicago San Francisco Lisbon London Madrid Mexico City
Milan New Delhi San Juan Seoul Singapore Sydney Toronto

Library of Congress Cataloging-in-Publication Data

DeGalan, Julie.
    Great Jobs for foreign language majors / by Julie DeGalan and Stephen Lambert — 3rd ed.
       p.   cm.
    ISBN 0-07-147614-8 (pb. : alk. paper)
    1. Language and languages—Vocational guidance.   2. Job hunting.   3. College
graduates—Employment.   I. Lambert, Stephen E.   II. Title.

P60D44   2007
650.14—dc20   ·   2006049247

1 2 3 4 5 6 7 8 9 10 11 12 13 14 15 16 17 18 19 20 21 22 DOC/DOC 0 9 8 7

ISBN-13: 978-0-07-147614-0
ISBN-10:   0-07-147614-8

McGraw-Hill books are available at special quantity discounts to use as premiums and sales promotions, or for use in corporate training programs. For more information, please write to the Director of Special Sales, Professional Publishing, McGraw-Hill, Two Penn Plaza, New York, NY 10121-2298. Or contact your local bookstore.

This book is printed on acid-free paper.

Contents

Introduction

Foreign Languages and the Educated Person

Defining just what makes a person "educated" is very difficult to do. However, although pundits disagree on many of the attributes that make someone truly educated, most would agree that the knowledge of at least one other language would be an important item on the list. If we review the history of the study of languages, we find that the study of Latin and Greek was, for many centuries, necessary for any scholar. As late as the mid-nineteenth century, an educated person could read in their original forms the works of great writers and thinkers, both ecclesiastical and secular. Virgil's *Aeneid*, Homer's *Iliad*, Aristotle's *Politics*, and Lady Murasaki Shikibu's *Tale of Genji* were all initially read and studied in their language of origin.

By the latter part of the nineteenth century, individual disciplines in the arts and sciences, such as chemistry, botany, and geology, began to evolve. Specialization in particular fields, including modern languages such as French and German, became necessary because it was no longer possible for an individual to be well read in many subject areas and stay current on rapid developments in industry, science, and medicine without knowledge of these more frequently used modern languages.

The study of European languages was brought to this country as part of a classic education. One could read and approach the literature, art, and architectural heritage of Europe more closely with an appreciation for, if not fluency in, one of the European languages. The "Grand Tour" of Europe was part of the finishing process in the educations of many upper-class young men and women; cultivating a knowledge of one of the Romance tongues was certainly helpful in that respect.

Studying a foreign language was often done out of strong social pressure to be appropriate, to know the correct things, to have a well-rounded education, to be well read, and to be worldly. As actual contact with other cultures was apt to be filtered and rather narrow, one would find it difficult to make a case that language study was for communication. It was done rather for self-improvement, often even for self-aggrandizement, and most often for social reasons.

Although we have mainly been talking about the late-eighteenth and early-nineteenth centuries, vestiges of this custom remain in junior year programs of study abroad or the simple desire of a new graduate to go abroad before settling down to a career. In fact, it is often mandatory for students in high school and, increasingly, junior high, to take classes in a foreign language. Today, throughout society, there continues to be a strong feeling that simply to have been exposed to foreign languages is a hallmark of good scholarship and a proper education.

Whatever the motivation might have been for language study early in our academic history, except for language scholars, there was not a rationale to support a tradition of *extended* foreign language study. Language study was principally a college occupation; it was not a lifelong occupation or concern but rather a requirement or a set of courses to accomplish. This is not true today.

A Harvard Business School professor coined the term "globalization" in 1983. Today, it is not simply a word or an abstract idea, but a way of life. Because the Earth seems to be shrinking, and we are increasingly having day-to-day contact with persons in countries around the globe, languages and studies of cultures are increasingly important. X-rays taken in a hospital in Boston, Massachusetts, are read in India; U.S. businesses have satellite offices in Germany, China, and Australia; and scientists of all stripes are conducting cutting-edge research in the jungles of South America and Africa and in the laboratories of Japan. Foreign languages are no longer the hobby of the affluent; they are the tool necessary for many to further their careers.

Language and Culture

When you study another language, you gain the understanding of language, not only the one being learned but also of your own. Foreign language study brings home the impact, the sensitivity, and the limitations of one's native language. It teaches volumes about the culture that uses the language being studied. Developing an understanding of a simple phrase in another language can explode the imagination. No mere translation can convey the true meaning of the phrase understood in its original expression.

In examining the Eskimo language, you'll find just one word for a motorized vehicle, meaning both an automobile and a motorcycle. You cannot distinguish between the two different machines by vocabulary, because historically the Eskimo culture was seldom confronted with motorized vehicles and had no need for such vocabulary. On the other hand, these people, who live in what others see as an almost monochromatic world of ice, have a multitude of words for snow. Wet snow; big snowflakes; dry, dusty snow; intermittent, spitting snow; snow that falls so fast there is no visibility—all have a term. Each culture reflects what is important to it in the language that it uses. Vocabulary teaches you far more than the correct word choice; it also betrays significance and cultural weight.

The growing interrelationships among the members of the world community call for sensitivity and understanding and not just of an emotive, affectionate nature. A sensitivity that is born out of an understanding and appreciation for another culture can best be achieved by knowing the language. Language gives us clues about how a people thinks and what a people values. While it is often mistakenly said that Japanese has no personal pronouns, it is true that Japanese is remarkably (and for students, frustratingly) free of references to personal pronouns. Who is doing the speaking and to whom that person is speaking is determined by the degree of honorific in the verb endings, and those degrees are many and subtle.

What do we learn from that? We certainly get the suggestion that aggressive self-promotion would be out of keeping with the Japanese character as would assertive references to others. Individuals in Japan approach each other delicately and subtly; they allow lots of maneuvering room for changes in tone, intention, and definitiveness. The implications for Americans interested in doing business with the Japanese are quite clear: We need people, both Japanese and American, who can help us bridge those differences and forge a relationship of meaning.

Americans are sometimes referred to as being culturally isolated but, like many blanket statements, this simply is not accurate. The United States is made up of citizens from countless nations, many of whom continue to speak their native languages in the home and with friends. We have whole communities of native speakers, so you might find a large cluster of Koreans in Los Angeles and an equally dense population of Cambodians in Lowell, Massachusetts. America is, in fact, a polyglot nation, and a careful look at its citizens would indicate that.

The so-called English language is also interwoven with non-English words, although most of us don't realize it. Dungaree is an Indian word; kindergarten is, of course, a German word. English uses a number of French words, too: croissant, esprit de corps, maître d', hors d'oeuvres, and chateaubriand. English constantly uses imports from many languages.

However, it is true that Americans do not have a good reputation for learning foreign languages, certainly not to the extent of other countries. One reason for this is the country's size and physical isolation from neighbors speaking a foreign tongue. There are some exceptions, however. In Vermont, New Hampshire, and Maine, which border the Canadian province of Quebec where French is spoken, many Americans of French-Canadian extraction speak French. In the Southwest, along the border of Mexico, Spanish is an important language.

Outside of these regions, unlike in European and Asian countries, which are in close proximity to other countries and whose citizens therefore learn several languages, Americans are comparatively isolated from other languages. Add to that the growing dominance of English in international business, and some Americans can justifiably feel less urgency about learning a foreign language. No matter where Americans go, it is easy to think that somebody who can speak a bit of English will always be right around the corner.

Without the foundation of some common language, communication is either crude gesture and pantomime or clinical data transfer devoid of any warmth, humor, or compassion. With shared language, we reach across enormous cultural boundaries. Knowledge of a language is certainly both a skill and an art that are well worth the many hours of study, language lab practice, travel, and reading to attain.

French, German, and Spanish

French has been in U.S. school curriculums for almost 150 years, and because of its associations with art, architecture, literature, cooking, and the world of diplomacy, it has remained a popular language option, even though the number of French-speaking citizens is far smaller than the number of German or Italian speakers Helping this dominance may be the fact that French literature remains a vital arena, as does French film. The French continue to play an important international role in other areas as well, including medicine, pharmacology, and science. Add to that the French zest for life and love of their own tongue, including their vigorous efforts to preserve its purity, and you can understand the language's staying power in this country.

German, the language traditionally associated with science, precision, and the military, has enjoyed a recent resurgence of popularity. Since the nineteenth century, it has been part of a good education. World War I and World War II did much to diminish the popularity of the study of German, and there still may be some residual feelings in older generations. Nevertheless, with the reunification of East and West Germany and Germany's participation in the European Community structure, it is anticipated that German will continue to be popular in foreign language training.

Spanish currently reigns as the most popular language, in terms of enrollment, being taught in the United States. Spanish language training often begins in the earliest grades. In some parts of the country, notably Florida, California, and the Southwest, there has been some controversy over the use of Spanish in public school systems. General debate continues in the media over what some see as a growing threat to the dominance of English in these parts of the country. Indeed, there is a major push among politically conservative groups to enact legislation declaring English the official language of the United States.

Because of the large number of Spanish-speaking households in the United States, many different types of businesses are trying to service these bilingual customers. For example, newspapers, ATMs, magazines, and TV and radio stations have targeted residents of certain communities by using languages other than English. Government agencies are also responding. Signage in some areas is in both English and Spanish—and oftentimes Japanese, Korean, Russian, or Polish!

Indeed, the languages French, German, and Spanish hardly begin to define the breadth of foreign language study being offered in this country. You can major in Swedish, Estonian, or Tibetan, and there are programs in Thai, Cantonese, Czech, Hebrew, Japanese, Chinese, Greek, or Laotian. And this list could go on and on. Language studies today are alive and well in the United States.

The Need for Foreign Languages

The exciting fact here is that foreign language study is needed now more than ever. The bonus for both the students and the teachers of foreign languages is that experiencing the language, using the language, and hearing and seeing it used are no longer confined to the classroom. Nor does it take a trip abroad. The world has grown closer and smaller, and that makes learning a language not just more meaningful, but also imperative.

The need for foreign language skills confronts you daily. In the political arena, world leaders often cannot retire alone to discuss important matters face-to-face and confidentially; interpreters must relay their communications. In equally significant arenas of economics, joint military operations, medicine, and science, global sharing is imperative and can be seriously impeded by the need for translation services. Each day the world community becomes ever more entwined in economic, political, social, and military combinations of states and countries. All work to do the best for their individual interests and at the same time make a contribution to overall harmony. The growing influence of the European Community, the increasing acceptance in Japan of foreign investment, the development of the

Chinese marketplace, the increasing openness of the Russian economy to entrepreneurship, foreign investment, and democratization all suggest exchange, movement, contact, and, above all else, a need for understanding.

The Internet has created a world at our fingertips. It allows us to tour the Louvre without leaving home, and we can even appropriate one of the great paintings in the galleries to display on our computer desktop! Sites from many countries offer the option of various languages with which to navigate their Web pages. We can now receive Italian television in our homes via satellite dishes, we can phone Thailand as easily as calling out of state, and we can correspond instantaneously using a fax machine with anyone in the world who has a machine to receive the message. The author recently planned a trip to Paris and with a few phone calls (in French) made hotel reservations, booked theater tickets, and even listened to a prerecorded listing (in English) of upcoming events in the City of Light. American stores are filled with products from around the world, many in the original packaging. U.S. cities abound with restaurants, coffeehouses, newspapers, radio and TV stations, and social centers for groups that are built around other languages. With so many dramatic examples of cultural interchange, it's easy to see why skilled foreign language graduates are in high demand.

Early language exposure invigorates the awareness of foreign language study by exposing students earlier to the process of acquiring another tongue. Research suggests that children who learn a second language are more creative and better at solving complex problems than those who do not. Studies have shown that bilingual children outperform their monolingual peers on both verbal and nonverbal tests of intelligence and tend to achieve higher scores on standardized tests.

Learning a foreign language increases children's acquisition of skills if started early in the educational process. The employment opportunities provided by the additional years of possible study are obvious: Adults who, as children, started learning a foreign language early in their school careers would excel over their peers in fluency, in text reading capability, and in transcription and translation skills. Japanese, for example, requires considerable years of study to master not only the spoken language but the 1,600 kanji (pictographs) necessary for basic literacy. There are tens of thousands more of these kanji needed for advanced reading. Beginning Japanese study in elementary school and continuing through high school and college could result in a verbal fluency and a mastery of written and printed Japanese not currently achieved by students who begin their Japanese studies in college.

Because the Japanese educational system requires twelve years of English study, there are far more native Japanese than there are American bilingual English/Japanese interpreters and translators. With an earlier start on the language, this would become a more competitive employment situation. The same holds true for other languages.

The Foreign Service of the United States uses an interesting definition of "useful" in categorizing language skill. For them, it is the ability to handle everyday speech, to read a newspaper, and to read and discuss a technical article in one particular field. Those skills are obvious, certainly, and can be gained through language institutes, preparation for graduate reading exams, or trade schools. They permit us to begin to make the real connections with people who speak that language and not our own. Important as that is, for many students of foreign languages it is not the most crucial. Many would say the real advantage of knowing a foreign language is the liberation of your mind.

Looking Ahead

The story of foreign language study has been one of shifting and deepening focus. Learning someone else's language is no longer a personal cultural adornment, but rather a signal of membership in and stewardship of the world community, which impacts us now with increasing frequency and urgency. The ground is shifting under our feet, and we will continue to see dramatic changes in the numbers of people learning foreign languages, in the use of and exposure to foreign languages in our own country, and, most important, in public opinion about the value and place of foreign language study.

The early indications of this shift have been mostly commercial. We are seeing a number of foreign languages used in American TV commercials, and the public is accepting it and enjoying it. Northwest Airlines has advertised in English over a duplicate copy of the ad in Japanese. It may be a background singer performing in French, it may be a German baker extolling an American product with subtitles, but whatever the use, it is no longer a shock to the formerly isolated English speakers of the United States to hear other languages being spoken and to see them in print. All of this serves to make us comfortable with what once was unusual and incomprehensible.

With the introduction of language studies to elementary school children, we can expect earlier foreign language acquisition and a greater number of languages learned in a lifetime. This is comparable to what has been happening in Europe for many generations, where inhabitants of small countries with relatively free border crossings found it imperative to learn several languages. Now, at least metaphorically, and with the aid of technology (television, telephones, e-mail, and transportation), our own proximity to other peoples, cultures, and languages has become much closer. We need to cross those borders more frequently and with greater understanding.

And it is not just the so-called traditional languages that are being introduced so early. Of course, Spanish, French, and German are popular, but so are Japanese, Chinese, Russian, and Italian. Computer technology is supporting these young language learners by speeding up the learning process. In addition, books and other aids will continue to become available for teaching and learning any number of languages at every educational level.

International correspondence is particularly difficult using ideogram-based languages. Recently developed technologies—in the form of computer programs and online services—have had a significant impact on world interactions and language learning. Translators of both Japanese and Chinese, two complex ideogram-based languages that use extensive pictographic vocabularies, have developed computer programs that "read" text or convert simpler syllabic text into pictographic symbols.

Perhaps one of the most useful technologies is any one of the many free online translation services available. Simply type in a word or phrase and with the push of a button you have a translation. This is particularly helpful for those learning languages as well as those in situations where a fluent, human translator isn't readily available.

The Power of Communication

Untold riches of art, literature, and tradition await as the growing mutual understanding of languages unfolds. We need this cultural interchange and the ideas it provides. Because U.S. culture, especially popular culture, is known the world over, how many of us can name the most popular Indian movie stars? Not many. That is particularly sad when we find out that the Indian movie industry is the largest in the world. And the same lack of knowledge exists about contemporary French novelists, Vietnamese poets, African artists, and countless other nations' contributions. All of this will be available to us in a world that shares languages.

Ultimately, we need to make the individual connections, whether it is two powerful leaders adjourning for a private conversation or a tourist and native sharing a cup of tea together. Each will find differences really not as vast as we once supposed when communication was obscured by the veil of a language we did not understand. The arenas may change; they may be political, social, economic, military, artistic, educational, or recreational, but the underlying need for individuals to understand each other does not change. Nothing can make that connection faster or more human than sharing a common language.

GREAT JOBS

FOR

Foreign Language Majors

PART ONE

THE JOB SEARCH

The Self-Assessment

Self-assessment is the process by which you begin to acknowledge your own particular blend of education, experiences, values, needs, and goals. It provides the foundation for career planning and the entire job search process. Self-assessment involves looking inward and asking yourself what can sometimes prove to be difficult questions. This self-examination should lead to an intimate understanding of your personal traits and values, consumption patterns and economic needs, longer-term goals, skill base, preferred skills, and underdeveloped skills.

You come to the self-assessment process knowing yourself well in some of these areas, but you may still be uncertain about other aspects. You may be well aware of your consumption patterns, but have you spent much time specifically identifying your longer-term goals or your personal values as they relate to work? No matter what level of self-assessment you have undertaken to date, it is now time to clarify all of these issues and questions as they relate to the job search.

The knowledge you gain in the self-assessment process will guide the rest of your job search. In this book, you will learn about all of the following tasks:

- Writing résumés and cover letters
- Researching careers and networking
- Interviewing and job offer considerations

In each of these steps, you will rely on and often return to the understanding gained through your self-assessment. Any individual seeking employment must be able and willing to express these facets of his or her personality to recruiters and interviewers throughout the job search. This communication allows you to show the world who you are so that together with employers you can determine whether there will be a workable match with a given job or career path.

How to Conduct a Self-Assessment

The self-assessment process goes on naturally all the time. People ask you to clarify what you mean, you make a purchasing decision, or you begin a new relationship. You react to the world and the world reacts to you. How you understand these interactions and any changes you might make because of them are part of the natural process of self-discovery. There is, however, a more comprehensive and efficient way to approach self-assessment with regard to employment.

Because self-assessment can become a complex exercise, we have distilled it into a seven-step process that provides an effective basis for undertaking a job search. The seven steps include the following:

1. Understanding your personal traits
2. Identifying your personal values
3. Calculating your economic needs
4. Exploring your longer-term goals
5. Enumerating your skill base
6. Recognizing your preferred skills
7. Assessing skills needing further development

As you work through your self-assessment, you might want to create a worksheet similar to the one shown in Exhibit 1.1, starting on the following page. Or you might want to keep a journal of the thoughts you have as you undergo this process. There will be many opportunities to revise your self-assessment as you start down the path of seeking a career.

Step 1   Understand Your Personal Traits

Each person has a unique personality that he or she brings to the job search process. Gaining a better understanding of your personal traits can help you evaluate job and career choices. Identifying these traits and then finding employment that allows you to draw on at least some of them can create a rewarding and fulfilling work experience. If potential employment doesn't allow you to use these preferred traits, it is important to decide whether you

Exhibit 1.1
SELF-ASSESSMENT WORKSHEET

Step 1. Understand Your Personal Traits
The personal traits that describe me are
(Include all of the words that describe you.)
The ten personal traits that most accurately describe me are
(List these ten traits.)

Step 2. Identify Your Personal Values
Working conditions that are important to me include
(List working conditions that would have to exist for you to accept a position.)
The values that go along with my working conditions are
(Write down the values that correspond to each working condition.)
Some additional values I've decided to include are
(List those values you identify as you conduct this job search.)

Step 3. Calculate Your Economic Needs
My estimated minimum annual salary requirement is
(Write the salary you have calculated based on your budget.)
Starting salaries for the positions I'm considering are
(List the name of each job you are considering and the associated starting salary.)

Step 4. Explore Your Longer-Term Goals
My thoughts on longer-term goals right now are
(Jot down some of your longer-term goals as you know them right now.)

Step 5. Enumerate Your Skill Base
The general skills I possess are
(List the skills that underlie tasks you are able to complete.)
The specific skills I possess are
(List more technical or specific skills that you possess, and indicate your level of expertise.)
General and specific skills that I want to promote to employers for the jobs I'm considering are
(List general and specific skills for each type of job you are considering.)

continued

Step 6. Recognize Your Preferred Skills

Skills that I would like to use on the job include

(List skills that you hope to use on the job, and indicate how often you'd like to use them.)

Step 7. Assess Skills Needing Further Development

Some skills that I'll need to acquire for the jobs I'm considering include

(Write down skills listed in job advertisements or job descriptions that you don't currently possess.)

I believe I can build these skills by

(Describe how you plan to acquire these skills.)

---

can find other ways to express them or whether you would be better off not considering this type of job. Interests and hobbies pursued outside of work hours can be one way to use personal traits you don't have an opportunity to draw on in your work. For example, if you consider yourself an outgoing person and the kinds of jobs you are examining allow little contact with other people, you may be able to achieve the level of interaction that is comfortable for you outside of your work setting. If such a compromise seems impractical or otherwise unsatisfactory, you probably should explore only jobs that provide the interaction you want and need on the job.

Many young adults who are not very confident about their employability will downplay their need for income. They will say, "Money is not all that important if I love my work." But if you begin to document exactly what you need for housing, transportation, insurance, clothing, food, and utilities, you will begin to understand that some jobs cannot meet your financial needs and it doesn't matter how wonderful the job is. If you have to worry each payday about bills and other financial obligations, you won't be very effective on the job. Begin now to be honest with yourself about your needs.

Begin the self-assessment process by creating an inventory of your personal traits. Make a list of as many words as possible to describe yourself. Words like *accurate, creative, future-oriented, relaxed,* or *structured* are just a few examples. In addition, you might ask people who know you well how they might describe you.

Focus on Selected Personal Traits. Of all the traits you identified, select the ten you believe most accurately describe you. Keep track of these ten traits.

Consider Your Personal Traits in the Job Search Process. As you begin exploring jobs and careers, watch for matches between your personal traits and the job descriptions you read. Some jobs will require many personal traits you know you possess, and others will not seem to match those traits.

A translator's work, for example, requires self-discipline, motivation, and an acute understanding of the text he or she is working with. Translators usually work alone, often at home, with limited opportunities to interact with others. An interpreter, on the other hand, interacts constantly with others. Interpreters need strong interpersonal and verbal skills and must be able to work under intense pressure. They must enjoy being in front of groups and must not mind interacting with individuals highly placed in government or business positions.

Your ability to respond to changing conditions, your decision-making ability, productivity, creativity, and verbal skills all have a bearing on your success in and enjoyment of your work life. To better guarantee success, be sure to take the time needed to understand these traits in yourself.

Step 2   Identify Your Personal Values

Your personal values affect every aspect of your life, including employment, and they develop and change as you move through life. Values can be defined as principles that we hold in high regard, qualities that are important and desirable to us. Some values aren't ordinarily connected to work (love, beauty, color, light, relationships, family, or religion), and others are (autonomy, cooperation, effectiveness, achievement, knowledge, and security). Our values determine, in part, the level of satisfaction we feel in a particular job.

Define Acceptable Working Conditions. One facet of employment is the set of working conditions that must exist for someone to consider taking a job.

Each of us would probably create a unique list of acceptable working conditions, but items that might be included on many people's lists are the amount of money you would need to be paid, how far you are willing to drive or travel, the amount of freedom you want in determining your own schedule, whether you would be working with people or data or things, and the types of tasks you would be willing to do. Your conditions might include statements of working conditions you will *not* accept; for example, you might not be willing to work at night or on weekends or holidays.

If you were offered a job tomorrow, what conditions would have to exist for you to realistically consider accepting the position? Take some time and make a list of these conditions.

Realize Associated Values. Your list of working conditions can be used to create an inventory of your values relating to jobs and careers you are exploring. For example, if one of your conditions stated that you wanted to earn at least $30,000 per year, the associated value would be financial gain. If another condition was that you wanted to work with a friendly group of people, the value that went along with that might be belonging or interaction with people.

Relate Your Values to the World of Work. As you read the job descriptions you come across either in this book, in newspapers and magazines, or online, think about the values associated with each position.

For example, the duties of a translator would include reading for complete comprehension in several languages, writing, and editing. Associated values are imagination, intellectual stimulation, and a desire for clear, accurate communication.

At least some of the associated values in the field you're exploring should match those you extracted from your list of working conditions. Take a second look at any values that don't match up. How important are they to you? What will happen if they are not satisfied on the job? Can you incorporate those personal values elsewhere? Your answers need to be brutally honest. As you continue your exploration, be sure to add to your list any additional values that occur to you.

Step 3   Calculate Your Economic Needs

Each of us grew up in an environment that provided for certain basic needs, such as food and shelter, and, to varying degrees, other needs that we now consider basic, such as cable television, e-mail, or an automobile. Needs such as privacy, space, and quiet, which at first glance may not appear to be monetary needs, may add to housing expenses and so should be considered as you examine your economic needs. For example, if you place a high value on a large, open living space for yourself, it would be difficult to satisfy that need without an associated high housing cost, especially in a densely populated city environment.

As you prepare to move into the world of work and become responsible for meeting your own basic needs, it is important to consider the salary you will need to be able to afford a satisfying standard of living. The three-step process outlined here will help you plan a budget, which in turn will allow you to evaluate the various career choices and geographic locations you are considering. The steps include (1) develop a realistic budget, (2) examine starting salaries, and (3) use a cost-of-living index.

Develop a Realistic Budget. Each of us has certain expectations for the kind of lifestyle we want to maintain. To begin the process of defining your economic needs, it will be helpful to determine what you expect to spend on routine monthly expenses. These expenses include housing, food, transportation, entertainment, utilities, loan repayments, and revolving charge accounts. You may not currently spend anything for certain items, but you probably will have to once you begin supporting yourself. As you develop this budget, be generous in your estimates, but keep in mind any items that could be reduced or eliminated. If you are not sure about the cost of a certain item, talk with family or friends who would be able to give you a realistic estimate.

If this is new or difficult for you, start to keep a log of expenses right now. You may be surprised at how much you actually spend each month for food or stamps or magazines. Household expenses and personal grooming items can often loom very large in a budget, as can auto repairs or home maintenance.

Income taxes must also be taken into consideration when examining salary requirements. State and local taxes vary, so it is difficult to calculate exactly the effect of taxes on the amount of income you need to generate. To roughly estimate the gross income necessary to generate your minimum annual salary requirement, multiply the minimum salary you have calculated by a factor of 1.35. The resulting figure will be an approximation of what your gross income would need to be, given your estimated expenses.

Examine Starting Salaries. Starting salaries for each of the career tracks are provided throughout this book. These salary figures can be used in conjunction with the cost-of-living index (discussed in the next section) to determine whether you would be able to meet your basic economic needs in a given geographic location.

Use a Cost-of-Living Index. If you are thinking about trying to get a job in a geographic region other than the one where you now live, understanding differences in the cost of living will help you come to a more informed decision about making a move. By using a cost-of-living index, you can compare salaries offered and the cost of living in different locations with what you know about the salaries offered and the cost of living in your present location.

Many variables are used to calculate the cost-of-living index. Often included are housing, groceries, utilities, transportation, health care, clothing, and entertainment expenses. Right now you do not need to worry about the details associated with calculating a given index. The main purpose of this exercise is to help you understand that pay ranges for entry-level positions may not vary greatly, but the cost of living in different locations *can* vary tremendously.

If you were working in Cleveland, Ohio, for example, and you were interested in working as a medical translator for a large medical center, you would plan on earning $40,000 annually. But let's say you're also thinking about moving to New York, Los Angeles, or Houston. You know you can live on $40,000 in Cleveland, but you want to be able to equal that salary in the other locations you're considering. How much will you have to earn in those locations to do this? Determining the cost of living for each city will show you.

There are many websites like Home Fair (homefair.com) that can assist you as you undertake this research. Entering the keywords "cost of living index" into any search engine will yield a variety of choices. Choose one site and look for options like "cost-of-living analysis" or "cost-of-living comparator." Some sites will ask you to register and/or pay for the information, but most sites are free. Follow the instructions provided and you will be able to create a table of information like the one shown here.

Job: Medical Translator

City	Base Amount	Equivalent Salary
Cleveland	$40,000	
New York		$52,348
Los Angeles		$38,581

At the time this comparison was done, you would have needed to earn $52,348 in New York and $38,581 in Los Angeles to match the buying power of $40,000 in Cleveland.

If you would like to determine whether it's financially worthwhile to make any of these moves, one more piece of information is needed: the salaries of medical translators in these other cities. One example of a website that contains job descriptions and salary information is Salary Expert (salaryexpert.com), which provides information based on area-specific government survey data. For example, a translator working in New York earns an average annual salary of $46,707. This means that half of those in this position would earn between $34,414 and $55,825. On the other hand, a translator working in Los Angeles earns an average annual salary of $38,479. Half of those in this position would earn between $28,351 and $45,990.

If you moved to New York City and secured employment as a medical translator, you would be able to maintain a lifestyle similar to the one you lead in Cleveland, although you may have to tighten the purse strings a bit. In Los Angeles, however, you could enjoy the same lifestyle and not have to worry about cutting back on any of your spending, since the earning power is basically the same as the cost-of-living index. Remember, these figures change all the time, so be sure to undertake your own calculations. If you would like to see the formula used, you can visit a website like Deloitte & Touche (deloitte.com).

Step 4   Explore Your Longer-Term Goals

There is no question that when we first begin working, our goals are to use our skills and education in a job that will reward us with employment, income, and status relative to the preparation we brought with us to this position. If we are not being paid as much as we feel we should for our level of education or if job demands don't provide the intellectual stimulation we had hoped for, we experience unhappiness and as a result often seek other employment.

Most jobs we consider "good" are those that fulfill our basic "lower-level" needs of security, food, clothing, shelter, income, and productive work. But even when our basic needs are met and our jobs are secure and productive, we as individuals are constantly changing. As we change, the demands and expectations we place on our jobs may change. Fortunately, some jobs grow and change with us, and this explains why some people are happy throughout many years in a job.

But more often people are bigger than the jobs they fill. We have more goals and needs than any job could satisfy. These are "higher-level" needs of self-esteem, companionship, affection, and an increasing desire to feel we are employing ourselves in the most effective way possible. Not all of these higher-level needs can be met through employment, but for as long as we are employed, we increasingly demand that our jobs play their part in moving us along the path to fulfillment.

Another obvious but important fact is that we change as we mature. Although our jobs also have the potential for change, they may not change as frequently or as markedly as we do. There are increasingly fewer one-job, one-employer careers; we must think about a work future that may involve voluntary or forced moves from employer to employer. Because of that very real possibility, we need to take advantage of the opportunities in each position we hold. Acquiring the skills and competencies associated with each position will keep us viable and attractive as employees. This is particularly true in a job market that not only is technology/computer dependent, but also is populated with more and more small, self-transforming organizations rather than the large, seemingly stable organizations of the past.

If you are considering a position in translating for the State Department, you would gain a far better perspective of this career if you could talk to an entry-level translator, a more senior and experienced department head, and finally, a senior Foreign Service Officer with a significant work history. Each will have a different perspective, unique concerns, and an individual set of values and priorities.

Step 5   Enumerate Your Skill Base

In terms of the job search, skills can be thought of as capabilities that can be developed in school, at work, or by volunteering and then used in specific job settings. Many studies have documented the kinds of skills that employers seek in entry-level applicants. For example, some of the most desired skills for individuals interested in the teaching profession are the ability to interact effectively with students one-on-one, to manage a classroom, to adapt to varying situations as necessary, and to get involved in school activities. Business employers have also identified important qualities, including enthusiasm for the employer's product or service, a businesslike mind, the ability to follow written or oral instructions, the ability to demonstrate self-control, the confidence to suggest new ideas, the ability to communicate with all members of a group, an awareness of cultural differences, and loyalty, to name just a few. You will find that many of these skills are also in the repertoire of qualities demanded in your college major.

To be successful in obtaining any given job, you must be able to demonstrate that you possess a certain mix of skills that will allow you to carry out the duties required by that job. This skill mix will vary a great deal from job to job; to determine the skills necessary for the jobs you are seeking, you can read job advertisements or more generic job descriptions, such as those found later in this book. If you want to be effective in the job search, you must directly show employers that you possess the skills needed to be successful in filling the position. These skills will initially be described on your résumé and then discussed again during the interview process.

Skills are either general or specific. To develop a list of skills relevant to employers, you must first identify the general skills you possess, then list specific skills you have to offer, and, finally, examine which of these skills employers are seeking.

Identify Your General Skills. Because you possess or will possess a college degree, employers will assume that you can read and write, perform certain basic computations, think critically, and communicate effectively. Employers will want to see that you have acquired these skills, and they will want to know which additional general skills you possess.

One way to begin identifying skills is to write an experiential diary. An experiential diary lists all the tasks you were responsible for completing for each job you've held and then outlines the skills required to do those tasks. You may list several skills for any given task. This diary allows you to distinguish between the tasks you performed and the underlying skills required to complete those tasks. Here's an example:

Tasks	Skills
Answering telephone	Effective use of language, clear diction, ability to direct inquiries, ability to solve problems
Waiting on tables	Poise under conditions of time and pressure, speed, accuracy, good memory, simultaneous completion of tasks, sales skills

For each job or experience you have participated in, develop a worksheet based on the example shown here. On a résumé, you may want to describe these skills rather than simply listing tasks. Skills are easier for the employer to appreciate, especially when your experience is very different from the employment you are seeking. In addition to helping you identify general skills, this experiential diary will prepare you to speak more effectively in an interview about the qualifications you possess.

Identify Your Specific Skills. It may be easier to identify your specific skills because you can definitely say whether you can speak other languages, program a computer, draft a map or diagram, or edit a document using appropriate symbols and terminology.

Using your experiential diary, identify the points in your history where you learned how to do something very specific, and decide whether you have a beginning, intermediate, or advanced knowledge of how to use that particular skill. Right now, be sure to list *every* specific skill you have, and don't consider whether you like using the skill. Write down a list of specific skills you have acquired and the level of competence you possess—beginning, intermediate, or advanced.

Relate Your Skills to Employers. You probably have thought about a couple of different jobs you might be interested in obtaining, and one way to begin relating the general and specific skills you possess to a potential employer's needs is to read actual advertisements for these types of positions (see Part Two for resources listing actual job openings).

For example, you might be interested in working as an online translator of website texts. A typical job listing might read, "Translate and input data into a web-based format. Extensive knowledge of computer applications a must. Prefer two to five years of experience in translation as well as computer science." Review a variety of print and online want ads that describe the job of an online translator or Web page operator to find additional information about what this sort of job might entail.

Begin building a comprehensive list of required skills with the first job description you read. Exploring advertisements for and descriptions of several types of related positions will reveal an important core of skills that are necessary for obtaining the type of work you're interested in. In building this list, include both general and specific skills.

Following is a sample list of skills needed to be successful as an online translator. These items were extracted from both general resources and actual job listings.

Job: Online Translator

General Skills	Specific Skills
Gather information	Prepare content in HTML format
Conduct research	Verify accuracy of colloquial translations
Enter data into computer	Launch online content
Work in casual environment	Lead or participate in
Meet deadlines	activities within a group

On a separate sheet of paper, try to generate a comprehensive list of required skills for at least one job you are considering.

The list of general skills that you develop for a given career path will be valuable for any number of jobs for which you might apply. Many of the specific skills would also be transferable to other types of positions. For example, preparing daily schedules is a required skill for leaders in any area.

Step 6   Recognize Your Preferred Skills

In the previous section you developed a comprehensive list of skills that relate to particular career paths that are of interest to you. You can now relate these to skills that you prefer to use. We all use a wide range of skills (some researchers say individuals have a repertoire of about five hundred skills), but we may not particularly be interested in using all of them in our work. There may be some skills that come to us more naturally or that we use successfully time and time again and that we want to continue to use; these are best described as our preferred skills. For this exercise use the list of skills that you created for the previous section, and decide which of them you are *most interested in using* in future work and how often you would like to use them. You might be interested in using some skills only occasionally, while others you would like to use more regularly. You probably also have skills that you hope you can use constantly.

As you examine job announcements, look for matches between this list of preferred skills and the qualifications described in the advertisements. These skills should be highlighted on your résumé and discussed in job interviews.

Step 7 Assess Skills Needing Further Development

Previously you compiled a list of general and specific skills required for given positions. You already possess some of these skills; those that remain to be developed are your underdeveloped skills.

If you are just beginning the job search, there may be gaps between the qualifications required for some of the jobs you're considering and the skills you possess. The thought of having to admit to and talk about these underdeveloped skills, especially in a job interview, is a frightening one. One way to put a healthy perspective on this subject is to target and relate your exploration of underdeveloped skills to the types of positions you are seeking. Recognizing these shortcomings and planning to overcome them with either on-the-job training or additional formal education can be a positive way to address the concept of underdeveloped skills.

On your worksheet or in your journal, make a list of up to five general or specific skills required for the positions you're interested in that you *don't currently possess*. For each item list an idea you have for specific action you could take to acquire that skill. Do some brainstorming to come up with possible actions. If you have a hard time generating ideas, talk to people currently working in this type of position, professionals in your college career services office, trusted friends, family members, or members of related professional associations.

In the chapter on interviewing, we will discuss in detail how to effectively address questions about underdeveloped skills. Generally speaking, though, employers want genuine answers to these types of questions. They want you to reveal "the real you," and they also want to see how you answer difficult questions. In taking the positive, targeted approach discussed previously, you show the employer that you are willing to continue to learn and that you have a plan for strengthening your job qualifications.

Use Your Self-Assessment

Exploring entry-level career options can be an exciting experience if you have good resources available and will take the time to use them. Can you effectively complete the following tasks?

1. Understand your personality traits and relate them to career choices
2. Define your personal values
3. Determine your economic needs
4. Explore longer-term goals
5. Understand your skill base
6. Recognize your preferred skills
7. Express a willingness to improve on your underdeveloped skills

If so, then you can more meaningfully participate in the job search process by writing a more effective résumé, finding job titles that represent work you are interested in doing, locating job sites that will provide the opportunity for you to use your strengths and skills, networking in an informed way, participating in focused interviews, getting the most out of follow-up contacts, and evaluating job offers to find those that create a good match between you and the employer. The remaining chapters in Part One guide you through these next steps in the job search process. For many job seekers, this process can take anywhere from three months to a year to implement. The time you will need to put into your job search will depend on the type of job you want and the geographic location where you'd like to work. Think of your effort as a job in itself, requiring you to set aside time each week to complete the needed work. Carefully undertaken efforts may reduce the time you need for your job search.

The Résumé and Cover Letter

The task of writing a résumé may seem overwhelming if you are unfamiliar with this type of document, but there are some easily understood techniques that can and should be used. This section was written to help you understand the purpose of the résumé, the different types of formats available, and how to write the sections that contain information traditionally found on a résumé. We will present examples and explanations that address questions frequently posed by people writing their first résumé or updating an old one.

Even within the formats and suggestions given, however, there are infinite variations. True, most follow one of the outlines suggested, but you should feel free to adjust the résumé to suit your needs and make it expressive of your life and experience.

Why Write a Résumé?

The purpose of a résumé is to convince an employer that you should be interviewed. Whether you're mailing, faxing, or e-mailing this document, you'll want to present enough information to show that you can make an immediate and valuable contribution to an organization. A résumé is not an in-depth historical or legal document; later in the job search process you may be asked to document your entire work history on an application form and attest to its validity. The résumé should, instead, highlight relevant information pertaining directly to the organization that will receive the document or to the type of position you are seeking.

We will discuss the chronological and digital résumés in detail here. Functional and targeted résumés, which are used much less often, are briefly discussed. The reasons for using one type of résumé over another and the typical format for each are addressed in the following sections.

The Chronological Résumé

The chronological résumé is the most common of the various résumé formats and therefore the format that employers are most used to receiving. This type of résumé is easy to read and understand because it details the chronological progression of jobs you have held. (See Exhibit 2.1.) It begins with your most recent employment and works back in time. If you have a solid work history or have experience that provided growth and development in your duties and responsibilities, a chronological résumé will highlight these achievements. The typical elements of a chronological résumé include the heading, a career objective, educational background, employment experience, activities, and references.

The Heading
The heading consists of your name, address, telephone number, and other means of contact. This may include a fax number, e-mail address, and your home-page address. If you are using a shared e-mail account or a parent's business fax, be sure to let others who use these systems know that you may receive important professional correspondence via these systems. You wouldn't want to miss a vital e-mail or fax! Likewise, if your résumé directs readers to a personal home page on the Web, be certain it's a professional personal home page designed to be viewed and appreciated by a prospective employer. This may mean making substantial changes in the home page you currently mount on the Web.

The Objective
Without a doubt the objective statement is the most challenging part of the résumé for most writers. Even for individuals who have decided on a career path, it can be difficult to encapsulate all they want to say in one or two brief sentences. For job seekers who are unfocused or unclear about their intentions, trying to write this section can inhibit the entire résumé writing process.

Keep the objective as short as possible and no longer than two short sentences.

Exhibit 2.1
CHRONOLOGICAL RÉSUMÉ

ANN WELSH
Green Grove Apartments, #30
2665 South University Drive
Athens, CA 30602
(404) 555-5555
awelsh@xxx.com
(until June 2007)
36 Pine Grove Avenue
Martinez, GA 30693
(404) 555-6666
(permanent address)

OBJECTIVE
To obtain a position as assistant director of international student affairs

EDUCATION
Bachelor of Arts in Spanish
University of Georgia, Athens
May 2007
Minor: Human Relations

HONORS/AWARDS
President's List, Fall Semester 2005, 2006
Who's Who Among Universities and Colleges, 2005–2007
Phi Kappa Phi National Honor Society

EXPERIENCE
Night Secretary: Gordon Research Conference, Augusta, Georgia 2005–
2006
Provided administrative support for conference evening activities. Extensive
international telephone work, some in Spanish, and international fax

continued

transmissions. Daily contact with international community of scientists. Received meritorious bonus each year.

Student Assistant: Dean of Student Affairs Office, University of Georgia, 2003–2005

A recurring financial aid–award position. Each year I added new duties and responsibilities, including booking appointments, touring guests around campus, assisting the dean with research, contacting students, and resolving problems. Constant contact with international students and their concerns.

Projectionist: Gordon Research Conference, Augusta, Georgia, 2002–2003

Summer position for world-renowned conference of international scientists. Provided all audiovisual setups for speakers from many different countries.

ACTIVITIES

Spanish Club, active member four years.

International Student Society sponsor. Helped a different international student each year meet friends and learn the campus.

REFERENCES

Both personal and professional references are available upon request.

Choose one of the following types of objective statement:

1. General Objective Statement

- An entry-level educational programming coordinator position

2. Position-Focused Objective

- To obtain the position of conference coordinator at State College

3. Industry-Focused Objective

- To begin a career as a sales representative in the cruise line industry

4. Summary of Qualifications Statement

A degree in French and several years of progressively increasing job responsibilities within the hospitality industry have prepared me to begin a career as a hotel manger trainee with an organization that values hard work and dedication.

Support Your Objective. A résumé that contains any one of these types of objective statements should then go on to demonstrate why you are qualified to get the position. Listing academic degrees can be one way to indicate qualifications. Another demonstration would be in the way previous experiences, both volunteer and paid, are described. Without this kind of documentation in the body of the résumé, the objective looks unsupported. Think of the résumé as telling a connected story about you. All the elements should work together to form a coherent picture that ideally should relate to your statement of objective.

Education

This section of your résumé should indicate the exact name of the degree you will receive or have received, spelled out completely with no abbreviations. The degree is generally listed after the objective, followed by the institution name and location, and then the month and year of graduation. This section could also include your academic minor, grade point average (GPA), and appearance on the Dean's List or President's List.

If you have enough space, you might want to include a section listing courses related to the field in which you are seeking work. The best use of a "related courses" section would be to list some course work that is not traditionally associated with the major. Perhaps you took several computer courses outside your degree that will be helpful and related to the job prospects you are entertaining. Several education section examples are shown here:

- Bachelor of Arts in Interdisciplinary Studies, a self-designed program concentrating in Spanish and Graphic Design; State College, Columbus, OH; May 2007
- Bachelor of Science Degree in French Education; University of Michigan, Ann Arbor, MI; December 2006

- Bachelor of Arts Degree in German; DePaul University, Chicago, IL; May 2007

An example of a format for a "related courses" section follows:

RELATED COURSES

Desktop Publishing	Advanced Composition
Computer Graphics	Creative Writing
Software Systems Design	Technical Writing

Experience

The experience section of your résumé should be the most substantial part and should take up most of the space on the page. Employers want to see what kind of work history you have. They will look at your range of experiences, longevity in jobs, and specific tasks you are able to complete. This section may also be called "work experience," "related experience," "employment history," or "employment." No matter what you call this section, some important points to remember are the following:

1. **Describe your duties** as they relate to the position you are seeking.
2. **Emphasize major responsibilities** and indicate increases in responsibility. Include all relevant employment experiences: summer, part-time, internships, cooperative education, or self-employment.
3. **Emphasize skills**, especially those that transfer from one situation to another. The fact that you coordinated a student organization, chaired meetings, supervised others, and managed a budget leads one to suspect that you could coordinate other things as well.
4. **Use descriptive job titles** that provide information about what you did. A "Student Intern" should be more specifically stated as, for example, "Magazine Operations Intern." "Volunteer" is also too general; a title such as "Peer Writing Tutor" would be more appropriate.
5. **Create word pictures** by using active verbs to start sentences. Describe *results* you have produced in the work you have done.

A limp description would say something such as the following: "My duties included helping with production, proofreading, and editing. I used a design and page layout program." An action statement would be stated as follows: "Coordinated and assisted in the creative marketing of brochures and seminar promotions, becoming proficient in Quark."

Remember, an accomplishment is simply a result, a final measurable product that people can relate to. A duty is not a result; it is an obligation—every job holder has duties. For an effective résumé, list as many results as you can. To make the most of the limited space you have and to give your description impact, carefully select appropriate and accurate descriptors.

Here are some traits that employers tell us they like to see:

- Teamwork
- Energy and motivation
- Learning and using new skills
- Versatility
- Critical thinking
- Understanding how profits are created
- Organizational acumen
- Communicating directly and clearly, in both writing and speaking
- Risk taking
- Willingness to admit mistakes
- High personal standards

Solutions to Frequently Encountered Problems

Repetitive Employment with the Same Employer
EMPLOYMENT: The Foot Locker, Portland, Oregon. Summer 2001, 2002, 2003. Initially employed in high school as salesclerk. Because of successful performance, asked to return next two summers at higher pay with added responsibility. Ranked as the #2 salesperson the first summer and #1 the next two summers. Assisted in arranging eye-catching retail displays; served as manager of other summer workers during owner's absence.

A Large Number of Jobs
EMPLOYMENT: Recent Hospitality Industry Experience: Affiliated with four upscale hotel/restaurant complexes (September 2001–February 2004), where I worked part- and full-time as a waiter, bartender, disc jockey, and bookkeeper to produce income for college.

Several Positions with the Same Employer

EMPLOYMENT: Coca-Cola Bottling Co., Burlington, Vermont, 2001–2004. In four years, I received three promotions, each with increased pay and responsibility.

Summer Sales Coordinator: Promoted to hire, train, and direct efforts of add-on staff of fifteen college-age route salespeople hired to meet summer peak demand for product.

Sales Administrator: Promoted to run home office sales desk, managing accounts and associated delivery schedules for professional sales force of ten people. Intensive phone work, daily interaction with all personnel, and strong knowledge of product line required.

Route Salesperson: Summer employment to travel and tourism industry sites that use Coke products. Met specific schedule demands, used good communication skills with wide variety of customers, and demonstrated strong selling skills. Named salesperson of the month for July and August of that year.

Questions Résumé Writers Often Ask

How Far Back Should I Go in Terms of Listing Past Jobs?

Usually, listing three or four jobs should suffice. If you did something back in high school that has a bearing on your future aspirations for employment, by all means list the job. As you progress through your college career, high school jobs will be replaced on the résumé by college employment.

Should I Differentiate Between Paid and Nonpaid Employment?

Most employers are not initially concerned about how much you were paid. They are eager to know how much responsibility you held in your past employment. There is no need to specify that your work was as a volunteer if you had significant responsibilities.

How Should I Represent My Accomplishments or Work-Related Responsibilities?

Succinctly, but fully. In other words, give the employer enough information to arouse curiosity but not so much detail that you leave nothing to the imagination. Besides, some jobs merit more lengthy explanations than others. Be sure to convey any information that can give an employer a better understanding of the depth of your involvement at work. Did you supervise others? How many? Did your efforts result in a more efficient operation? How much did you increase efficiency? Did you handle a budget? How much? Were you promoted in a short time? Did you work two jobs at once or fifteen hours per week after high school? Where appropriate, quantify.

Should the Work Section Always Follow the Education Section on the Résumé?

Always lead with your strengths. If your education closely relates to the employment you now seek, put this section after the objective. If your education does not closely relate but you have a surplus of good work experiences, consider reversing the order of your sections to lead with employment, followed by education.

How Should I Present My Activities, Honors, Awards, Professional Societies, and Affiliations?

This section of the résumé can add valuable information for an employer to consider if used correctly. The rule of thumb for information in this section is to include only those activities that are in some way relevant to the objective stated on your résumé. If you can draw a valid connection between your activities and your objective, include them; if not, leave them out.

Professional affiliations and honors should all be listed; especially important are those related to your job objective. Social clubs and activities need not be a part of your résumé unless you hold a significant office or you are looking for a position related to your membership. Be aware that most prospective employers' principal concerns are related to your employability, not your social life. If you have any, publications can be included as an addendum to your résumé.

How Should I Handle References?

The use of references is considered a part of the interview process, and they should never be listed on a résumé. You would always provide references to a potential employer if requested to, so it is not even necessary to include this section on the résumé if space does not permit. If space is available, it is acceptable to include the following statement:

- References furnished upon request.

The Functional Résumé

The functional résumé departs from a chronological résumé in that it organizes information by specific accomplishments in various settings: previous jobs, volunteer work, associations, and so forth. This type of résumé permits you to stress the substance of your experiences rather than the position titles you have held. You should consider using a functional résumé if you have held a series of similar jobs that relied on the same skills or abilities. There are many good books in which you can find examples of functional résumés, including *How to Write a Winning Resume* or *Resumes Made Easy*.

The Targeted Résumé

The targeted résumé focuses on specific work-related capabilities you can bring to a given position within an organization. Past achievements are listed to highlight your capabilities and the work history section is abbreviated.

Digital Résumés

Today's employers have to manage an enormous number of résumés. One of the most frequent complaints the writers of this series hear from students is the failure of employers to even acknowledge the receipt of a résumé and cover letter. Frequently, the reason for this poor response or nonresponse is the volume of applications received for every job. In an attempt to better manage the considerable labor investment involved in processing large numbers of résumés, many employers are requiring digital submission of résumés. There are two types of digital résumés: those that can be e-mailed or posted to a website, called *electronic résumés*, and those that can be "read" by a computer, commonly called *scannable résumés*. Though the format may be a bit different from the traditional "paper" résumé, the goal of both types of digital résumés is the same—to get you an interview! These résumés must be designed to be "technologically friendly." What that basically means to you is that they should be free of graphics and fancy formatting. (See Exhibit 2.2.)

Electronic Résumés
Sometimes referred to as plain-text résumés, electronic résumés are designed to be e-mailed to an employer or posted to one of many commercial Internet databases such as CareerMosaic.com, America's Job Bank (ajb.dni.us), or Monster.com.

Exhibit 2.2
DIGITAL RÉSUMÉ

SARAH McDOUGLE
117 Stetson Avenue
Boston, MA 02459
(859) 555-5478
sarahmc@xxx.com

KEYWORD SUMMARY
B.S. Computer Science, B.A. Japanese, C++, HTML, MS Office,
   Programmer, Interpreter, Translator, Web Page Design

EDUCATION
Bachelor of Science, Computer Science, 2007
Bachelor of Arts, Japanese, 2005
St. Xavier College, Boston, MA

EXPERIENCE
Support desk, St. Xavier College, 2004-2006
* Maintained computer systems in computer lab
* Installed application and performed troubleshooting
* Instructed students on application and systems
* Provided Japanese services as necessary to diverse student body
Programmer (intern), LearnTech Services, 2003
* Wrote instructional programs in both English and Japanese
* Corrected errors in prewritten programs using C++
* Altered existing programs to fit user needs

COMMUNICATION SKILLS
Served as a vice president of Computer Science Society
Received As in technical writing and speech class
Served as tutor for ESL students

REFERENCES
Available upon request
Willing to relocate

Some technical considerations:

- Electronic résumés must be written in American Standard Code for Information Interchange (ASCII), which is simply a plain-text format. These characters are universally recognized so that every computer can accurately read and understand them. To create an ASCII file of your current résumé, open your document, then save it as a text or ASCII file. This will eliminate all formatting. Edit as needed using your computer's text editor application.
- Use a standard-width typeface. Courier is a good choice because it is the font associated with ASCII in most systems.
- Use a font size of 11 to 14 points. A 12-point font is considered standard.
- Your margin should be left-justified.
- Do not exceed sixty-five characters per line because the word-wrap function doesn't operate in ASCII.
- Do not use boldface, italics, underlining, bullets, or various font sizes. Instead, use asterisks, plus signs, or all capital letters when you want to emphasize something.
- Avoid graphics and shading.
- Use as many "keywords" as you possibly can. These are words or phrases usually relating to skills or experience that either are specifically used in the job announcement or are popular buzzwords in the industry.
- Minimize abbreviations.
- Your name should be the first line of text.
- Conduct a "test run" by e-mailing your résumé to yourself and a friend before you send it to the employer. See how it transmits, and make any changes you need to. Continue to test it until it's exactly how you want it to look.
- Unless an employer specifically requests that you send the résumé in the form of an attachment, don't. Employers can encounter problems opening a document as an attachment, and there are always viruses to consider.
- Don't forget your cover letter. Send it along with your résumé as a single message.

Scannable Résumés

Some companies are relying on technology to narrow the candidate pool for available job openings. Electronic Applicant Tracking uses imaging to scan, sort, and store résumé elements in a database. Then, through OCR (Optical Character Recognition) software, the computer scans the résumés for keywords and phrases. To have the best chance at getting an interview, you want to increase the number of "hits"—matches of your skills, abilities, experience, and education to those the computer is scanning for—your résumé will get. You can see how critical using the right keywords is for this type of résumé.

Technical considerations include:

- Again, do not use boldface (newer systems may be able to read this, but many older ones won't), italics, underlining, bullets, shading, graphics, or multiple font sizes. Instead, for emphasis, use asterisks, plus signs, or all capital letters. Minimize abbreviations.
- Use a popular typeface such as Courier, Helvetica, Ariel, or Palatino. Avoid decorative fonts.
- Font size should be between 11 and 14 points.
- Do not compress the spacing between letters.
- Use horizontal and vertical lines sparingly; the computer may misread them as the letters *L* or *I*.
- Left-justify the text.
- Do not use parentheses or brackets around telephone numbers, and be sure your phone number is on its own line of text.
- Your name should be the first line of text and on its own line. If your résumé is longer than one page, be sure to put your name on the top of all pages.
- Use a traditional résumé structure. The chronological format may work best.
- Use nouns that are skill-focused, such as *management, writer,* and *programming.* This is different from traditional paper résumés, which use action-oriented verbs.
- Laser printers produce the finest copies. Avoid dot-matrix printers.
- Use standard, light-colored paper with text on one side only. Since the higher the contrast, the better, your best choice is black ink on white paper.
- Always send original copies. If you must fax, set the fax on fine mode, not standard.
- Do not staple or fold your résumé. This can confuse the computer.
- Before you send your scannable résumé, be certain the employer uses this technology. If you can't determine this, you may want to send two versions (scannable and traditional) to be sure your résumé gets considered.

Résumé Production and Other Tips

An ink-jet printer is the preferred option for printing your résumé. Begin by printing just a few copies. You may find a small error or you may simply want to make some changes, and it is less frustrating and less expensive if you print in small batches.

Résumé paper color should be carefully chosen. You should consider the types of employers who will receive your résumé and the types of positions for which you are applying. Use white or ivory paper for traditional or conservative employers or for higher-level positions.

Black ink on sharp, white paper can be harsh on the reader's eyes. Think about an ivory or cream paper that will provide less contrast and be easier to read. Pink, green, and blue tints should generally be avoided.

Many résumé writers buy packages of matching envelopes and cover sheet stationery that, although not absolutely necessary, help convey a professional impression.

If you'll be producing many cover letters at home, be sure you have high-quality printing equipment. Learn standard envelope formats for business, and retain a copy of every cover letter you send out. You can use the copies to take notes of any telephone conversations that may occur.

If attending a job fair, either carry a briefcase or place your résumé in a nicely covered legal-size pad holder.

The Cover Letter

The cover letter provides you with the opportunity to tailor your résumé by telling the prospective employer how you can be a benefit to the organization. It allows you to highlight aspects of your background that are not already discussed in your résumé and that might be especially relevant to the organization you are contacting or to the position you are seeking. Every résumé should have a cover letter enclosed when you send it out. Unlike the résumé, which may be mass-produced, a cover letter is most effective when it is individually prepared and focused on the particular requirements of the organization in question.

A good cover letter should supplement the résumé and motivate the reader to review the résumé. The format shown in Exhibit 2.3 (see page 34) is only a suggestion to help you decide what information to include in a cover letter.

Begin the cover letter with your street address six lines down from the top. Leave three to five lines between the date and the name of the person to whom you are addressing the cover letter. Make sure you leave one blank line between the salutation and the body of the letter and between paragraphs. After typing "Sincerely," leave four blank lines and type your name.

This should leave plenty of room for your signature. A sample cover letter is shown in Exhibit 2.4 on page 35.

The following guidelines will help you write good cover letters:

1. Be sure to type your letter neatly; ensure there are no misspellings.
2. Avoid unusual typefaces, such as script.
3. Address the letter to an individual, using the person's name and title. To obtain this information, call the company. If answering a blind newspaper advertisement, address the letter "To Whom It May Concern" or omit the salutation.
4. Be sure your cover letter directly indicates the position you are applying for and tells why you are qualified to fill it.
5. Send the original letter, not a photocopy, with your résumé. Keep a copy for your records.
6. Make your cover letter no more than one page.
7. Include a phone number where you can be reached.
8. Avoid trite language and have someone read the letter over to react to its tone, content, and mechanics.
9. For your own information, record the date you send out each letter and résumé.

Exhibit 2.3
COVER LETTER FORMAT

Your Street Address
Your Town, State, Zip
Phone Number
Fax Number
E-mail

Date

Name
Title
Organization
Address

Dear _____:

First Paragraph. In this paragraph state the reason for the letter, name the specific position or type of work you are applying for, and indicate from which resource (career services office, website, newspaper, contact, employment service) you learned of this opening. The first paragraph can also be used to inquire about future openings.

Second Paragraph. Indicate why you are interested in this position, the company, or its products or services and what you can do for the employer. If you are a recent graduate, explain how your academic background makes you a qualified candidate. Try not to repeat the same information found in the résumé.

Third Paragraph. Refer the reader to the enclosed résumé for more detailed information.

Fourth Paragraph. In this paragraph say what you will do to follow up on your letter. For example, state that you will call by a certain date to set up an interview or to find out if the company will be recruiting in your area. Finish by indicating your willingness to answer any questions the recipient may have. Be sure you have provided your phone number.

Sincerely,

Type your name
Enclosure

Exhibit 2.4
SAMPLE COVER LETTER

143 Random Way
Shreveport, LA 71130
(318) 555-5555
jsmith@xxx.com

November 29, 2007

Kimberly Crane
Director of Personnel
ACME Distributors
279 Main Street
Shreveport, LA 71130

Dear Ms. Crane:

In May 2008, I will graduate from Louisiana State University with a bachelor of arts degree in French. I read of your sales opening on the *Times* website, and I am very interested in the possibilities it offers. I am writing to explore the opportunity for employment with your company.

The ad indicated that you were looking for enthusiastic individuals with exceptional communication skills. I believe that I possess those qualities. Through my job as a waitress at a busy diner, I have learned the importance of having high energy and maintaining a positive attitude toward customers. In addition to the various marketing classes in my academic program, I felt it important to enroll in some communication courses, such as human communication skills, interpersonal communication, and public speaking. These courses helped me to become comfortable in my interactions with other people, and they taught me how to communicate clearly. These characteristics will help me to represent ACME in a professional and enthusiastic manner.

As you will see by my enclosed résumé, I was an admissions representative for three years of college. This position provided me with sales experience in that campus tours involved a certain degree of persuasive presentation of the college and its features to prospective students.

continued

I would like to meet with you to discuss how my education and experience would be consistent with your needs. I will contact your office next week to discuss the possibility of an interview. In the meantime, if you have any questions or require additional information, please contact me at home, (318) 555-5555.

Sincerely,

Jennifer Smith

Enclosure

Researching Careers
and Networking

What do they call the job you want? One reason for confusion is perhaps a mistaken assumption that a college education provides job training. In most cases it does not. Of course, applied fields such as engineering, management, or education provide specific skills for the workplace as well as an education. Regardless, your overall college education exposes you to numerous fields of study and teaches you quantitative reasoning, critical thinking, writing, and speaking, all of which can be successfully applied to a number of different job fields. But it still remains up to you to choose a job field and to learn how to articulate the benefits of your education in a way the employer will appreciate.

Collect Job Titles

The world of employment is a complex place, so you need to become a bit of an explorer and adventurer and be willing to try a variety of techniques to develop a list of possible occupations that might use your talents and

---

One common question a career counselor encounters is, "What can I do with my degree?" Foreign language majors often struggle with this problem because, unlike their fellow students in more applied fields, such as accounting, computer science, or health and physical education, there is real confusion about just what kinds of jobs can be done with a foreign language degree and what kinds of organizations hire for those positions. An accounting major becomes an accountant. A computer science major can apply for a job as a data analyst. But what does a foreign language major become?

---

education. You might find computerized interest inventories, reference books and other sources, and classified ads helpful in this respect. Once you have a list of possibilities that you are interested in and qualified for, you can move on to find out what kinds of organizations have these job titles.

Computerized Interest Inventories

One way to begin collecting job titles is to identify a number of jobs that call for your degree and the particular skills and interests you identified as part of the self-assessment process. There are excellent interactive career-guidance programs on the market to help you produce such selected lists of possible job titles. Most of these are available at colleges and at some larger town and city libraries. Two of the industry leaders are *CHOICES* and *DIS-COVER*. Both allow you to enter interests, values, educational background, and other information to produce lists of possible occupations and industries. Each of the resources listed here will produce different job title lists. Some job titles will appear again and again, while others will be unique to a particular source. Investigate all of them!

Reference Sources

Books on the market that may be available through your local library or career counseling office also suggest various occupations related to specific majors. The following are only a few of the many good books on the market: *The College Board Guide to 150 Popular College Majors* and *College Majors and Careers: A Resource Guide for Effective Life Planning* both by Paul Phifer, and *Kaplan's What to Study: 101 Fields in a Flash*. All of these books list possible job titles within the academic major.

Not every employer seeking to hire a translator may be equally desirable to you. Some employment environments may be more attractive to you than others. A foreign language major considering translating as a profession could do that in a major corporation, a government agency, a medical institution, a financial organization, or a court system. Each of these environments presents a different "culture" with associated norms in the place of work, the subject matter of interest, and the backgrounds of its employees. Although the job titles may be the same, not all locations may present the same "fit" for you.

If you majored in foreign languages and enjoyed the in-class presentations you made as part of your degree and developed some good writing skills, you might naturally think law is a possibility for you. You may consider graduate school and a J.D. degree. But foreign language majors with these skills also become government managers, advertising executives, trainers, public relations practitioners, and bank officers. Each of these job titles can also be found in a number of different settings.

Each job title deserves your consideration. Like removing the layers of an onion, the search for job titles can go on and on! As you spend time doing this activity, you are actually learning more about the value of your degree. What's important in your search at this point is not to become critical or selective but rather to develop as long a list of possibilities as you can. Every source used will help you add new and potentially exciting jobs to your growing list.

Classified Ads

It has been well publicized that the classified ad section of the newspaper represents only a small fraction of the current job market. Nevertheless, the weekly classified ads can be a great help to you in your search. Although they may not be the best place to look for a job, they can teach you a lot about the job market. Classified ads provide a good education in job descriptions, duties, responsibilities, and qualifications. In addition, they provide insight into which industries are actively recruiting and some indication of the area's employment market. This is particularly helpful when seeking a position in a specific geographic area and/or a specific field. For your purposes, classified ads are a good source for job titles to add to your list.

Read the Sunday classified ads in a major market newspaper for several weeks in a row. Cut and paste all the ads that interest you and seem to call for something close to your education, skills, experience, and interests. Remember that classified ads are written for what an organization *hopes* to find; you don't have to meet absolutely every criterion. However, if certain requirements are stated as absolute minimums and you cannot meet them, it's best not to waste your time and that of the employer.

The weekly classified want ads exercise is important because these jobs are out in the marketplace. They truly exist, and people with your qualifications are being sought to apply. What's more, many of these advertisements describe the duties and responsibilities of the job advertised and give you a beginning sense of the challenges and opportunities such a position presents. Some will indicate salary, and that will be helpful as well. This information will better define the jobs for you and provide some good material for possible interviews in that field.

Explore Job Descriptions

Once you've arrived at a solid list of possible job titles that interest you and for which you believe you are somewhat qualified, it's a good idea to do some research on each of these jobs. The preeminent source for such job information is the *Dictionary of Occupational Titles*, or *DOT* (wave.net/upg/immigration/dot_index.html). This directory lists every conceivable job and provides excellent up-to-date information on duties and responsibilities, interactions with associates, and day-to-day assignments and tasks. These descriptions provide a thorough job analysis, but they do not consider the possible employers or the environments in which a job may be performed. So, although a position as public relations officer may be well defined in terms of duties and responsibilities, it does not explain the differences in doing public relations work in a college or a hospital or a factory or a bank. You will need to look somewhere else for work settings.

Learn More About Possible Work Settings

After reading some job descriptions, you may choose to edit and revise your list of job titles once again, discarding those you feel are not suitable and keeping those that continue to hold your interest. Or you may wish to keep your list intact and see where these jobs may be located. For example, if you are interested in public relations and you appear to have those skills and the requisite education, you'll want to know which organizations do public relations. How can you find that out? How much income does someone in public relations make a year and what is the employment potential for the field of public relations?

To answer these and many other questions about your list of job titles, we recommend you try any of the following resources: *Careers Encyclopedia*, the professional societies and resources found throughout this book, *College to Career: The Guide to Job Opportunities*, and the *Occupational Outlook Handbook* (http://stats.bls.gov/ocohome.htm). Each of these resources, in a different way, will help to put the job titles you have selected into an employer context. Perhaps the most extensive discussion is found in the *Occupational Outlook Handbook*, which gives a thorough presentation of the nature of the work, the working conditions, employment statistics, training, other qualifications, and advancement possibilities as well as job outlook and earnings. Related occupations are also detailed, and a select bibliography is provided to help you find additional information.

Continuing with our public relations example, your search through these reference materials would teach you that the public relations jobs you find attractive are available in larger hospitals, financial institutions, most corporations (both consumer goods and industrial goods), media organizations, and colleges and universities.

Networking

Networking is the process of deliberately establishing relationships to get career-related information or to alert potential employers that you are available for work. Networking is critically important to today's job seeker for two reasons: It will help you get the information you need, and it can help you find out about *all* of the available jobs.

Get the Information You Need

Networkers will review your résumé and give you feedback on its effectiveness. They will talk about the job you are looking for and give you a candid appraisal of how they see your strengths and weaknesses. If they have a good sense of the industry or the employment sector for that job, you'll get their feelings on future trends in the industry as well. Some networkers will be very forthcoming about salaries, job-hunting techniques, and suggestions for your job search strategy. Many have been known to place calls right from the interview desk to friends and associates who might be interested in you. Each networker will make his or her own contribution, and each will be valuable.

Because organizations must evolve to adapt to current global market needs, the information provided by decision makers within various organizations will be critical to your success as a new job market entrant. For example, you might learn about the concept of virtual organizations from a networker. Virtual organizations coordinate economic activity to deliver value to customers by using resources outside the traditional boundaries of the organization. This concept is being discussed and implemented by chief executive officers of many organizations, including Ford Motor, Dell, and IBM. Networking can help you find out about this and other trends currently affecting the industries under your consideration.

Find Out About All of the Available Jobs

Not every job that is available at this very moment is advertised for potential applicants to see. This is called the *hidden job market*. Only 15 to 20 percent of all jobs are formally advertised, which means that 80 to 85 percent of available jobs do not appear in published channels. Networking will help you become more knowledgeable about all the employment opportunities available during your job search period.

Although someone you might talk to today doesn't know of any openings within his or her organization, tomorrow or next week or next month an opening may occur. If you've taken the time to show an interest in and knowledge of their organization, if you've shown the company representative how you can help achieve organizational goals and that you can fit into the organization, you'll be one of the first candidates considered for the position.

Networking: A Proactive Approach

Networking is a proactive rather than a reactive approach. You, as a job seeker, are expected to initiate a certain level of activity on your own behalf; you cannot afford to simply respond to jobs listed in the newspaper. Being proactive means building a network of contacts that includes informed and interested decision makers who will provide you with up-to-date knowledge of the current job market and increase your chances of finding out about employment opportunities appropriate for your interests, experience, and level of education. An old axiom of networking says, "You are only two phone calls away from the information you need." In other words, by talking to enough people, you will quickly come across someone who can offer you help.

Preparing to Network

In deliberately establishing relationships, maximize your efforts by organizing your approach. Five specific areas in which you can organize your efforts include reviewing your self-assessment, reviewing your research on job sites and organizations, deciding who you want to talk to, keeping track of all your efforts, and creating your self-promotion tools.

Review Your Self-Assessment

Your self-assessment is as important a tool in preparing to network as it has been in other aspects of your job search. You have carefully evaluated your personal traits, personal values, economic needs, longer-term goals, skill base, preferred skills, and underdeveloped skills. During the networking process you will be called upon to communicate what you know about yourself and relate it to the information or job you seek. Be sure to review the exercises that you completed in the self-assessment section of this book in preparation for networking. We've explained that you need to assess which skills you have acquired from your major that are of general value to an employer; be ready to express those in ways he or she can appreciate as useful in the organizations.

Review Research on Job Sites and Organizations

In addition, individuals assisting you will expect that you'll have at least some background information on the occupation or industry of interest to you. Refer to the appropriate sections of this book and other relevant publications to acquire the background information necessary for effective networking. They'll explain how to identify not only the job titles that might be of interest to you but also which kinds of organizations employ people to do that job. You will develop some sense of working conditions and expectations about duties and responsibilities—all of which will be of help in your networking interviews.

Decide Who You Want to Talk To

Networking cannot begin until you decide who you want to talk to and, in general, what type of information you hope to gain from your contacts. Once you know this, it's time to begin developing a list of contacts. Five useful sources for locating contacts are described here.

College Alumni Network. Most colleges and universities have created a formal network of alumni and friends of the institution who are particularly interested in helping currently enrolled students and graduates of their alma mater gain employment-related information.

It is usually a simple process to make use of an alumni network. Visit your college's website and locate the alumni office and/or your career center. Either or both sites will have information about your school's alumni network. You'll be provided with information on shadowing experiences, geographic information, or those alumni offering job referrals. If you don't find what you're looking for, don't hesitate to phone or e-mail your career center and ask what they can do to help you connect with an alum.

Alumni networkers may provide some combination of the following services: day-long shadowing experiences, telephone interviews, in-person interviews, information on relocating to given geographic areas, internship information, suggestions on graduate school study, and job vacancy notices.

Present and Former Supervisors. If you believe you are on good terms with present or former job supervisors, they may be an excellent resource for providing information or directing you to appropriate resources that would have information related to your current interests and needs. Additionally, these supervisors probably belong to professional organizations that they might be willing to utilize to get information for you.

Employers in Your Area. Although you may be interested in working in a geographic location different from the one where you currently reside, don't overlook the value of the knowledge and contacts those around you are able to provide. Use the local telephone directory and newspaper to identify the types of organizations you are thinking of working for or professionals who have the kinds of jobs you are interested in. Recently, a call made to a local hospital's financial administrator for information on working in health-care financial administration yielded more pertinent information on training seminars, regional professional organizations, and potential employment sites than a national organization was willing to provide.

Employers in Geographic Areas Where You Hope to Work. If you are thinking about relocating, identifying prospective employers or informational contacts in the new location will be critical to your success. Here are some tips for online searching. First, use a "metasearch engine" to get the most out of your search. Metasearch engines combine several engines into one powerful tool. We frequently use dogpile.com and metasearch.com for this purpose. Try using the city and state as your keywords in a search. *New Haven, Connecticut* will bring you to the city's website with links to the chamber of commerce, member businesses, and other valuable resources. By using looksmart.com you can locate newspapers in any area, and they, too, can provide valuable insight before you relocate. Of course, both dogpile and metasearch can lead you to yellow and white page directories in areas you are considering.

Professional Associations and Organizations. Professional associations and organizations can provide valuable information in several areas: career paths that you might not have considered, qualifications relating to those career choices, publications that list current job openings, and workshops or seminars that will enhance your professional knowledge and skills. They can also be excellent sources for background information on given industries: their health, current problems, and future challenges.

There are several excellent resources available to help you locate professional associations and organizations that would have information to meet your needs. Two especially useful publications are the *Encyclopedia of Associations* and *National Trade and Professional Associations of the United States.*

Keep Track of All Your Efforts

It can be difficult, almost impossible, to remember all the details related to each contact you make during the networking process, so you will want to develop a record-keeping system that works for you. Formalize this process by using your computer to keep a record of the people and organizations you want to contact. You can simply record the contact's name, address, and telephone number, and what information you hope to gain.

You could record this as a simple Word document and you could still use the "Find" function if you were trying to locate some data and could only recall the firm's name or the contact's name. If you're comfortable with database management and you have some database software on your computer, then you can put information at your fingertips even if you have only the zip code! The point here is not technological sophistication but good record keeping.

Once you have created this initial list, it will be helpful to keep more detailed information as you begin to actually make the contacts. Those details should include complete contact information, the date and content of each contact, names and information for additional networkers, and required follow-up. Don't forget to send a letter thanking your contact for his or her time! Your contact will appreciate your recall of details of your meetings and conversations, and the information will help you to focus your networking efforts.

Create Your Self-Promotion Tools

There are two types of promotional tools that are used in the networking process. The first is a résumé and cover letter, and the second is a one-minute "infomercial," which may be given over the telephone or in person.

Techniques for writing an effective résumé and cover letter are discussed in Chapter 2. Once you have reviewed that material and prepared these important documents, you will have created one of your self-promotion tools.

The one-minute infomercial will demand that you begin tying your interests, abilities, and skills to the people or organizations you want to network with. Think about your goal for making the contact to help you understand what you should say about yourself. You should be able to express yourself easily and convincingly. If, for example, you are contacting an alumnus of your institution to obtain the names of possible employment sites in a distant city, be prepared to discuss why you are interested in moving to that location, the types of jobs you are interested in, and the skills and abilities you possess that will make you a qualified candidate.

To create a meaningful one-minute infomercial, write it out, practice it as if it will be a spoken presentation, rewrite it, and practice it again if necessary until expressing yourself comes easily and is convincing.

Here's a simplified example of an infomercial for use over the telephone:

Hello, Ms. Regan? My name is Ruth Fowler. I am a recent graduate of Polytechnic University, and I would like to enter the import/export field. I was a French major in college and feel confident that I have many of the skills that are valued in import/export beyond my fluency in French. I have good computational skills, computer expertise, and I am confident of my writing and speaking abilities in English as well. What's more, I work well under pressure. I have read that that can be a real advantage in your field!

> I'm calling you because I still need more information in this area. I'm hoping you'll have the time to sit down with me for about half an hour and discuss your perspective on import/export careers with me. There are so many possible industries that are involved in import/export, and I am seeking some advice on which of those settings might be the best for my particular combination of skills and experiences.
>
> Would you be willing to do that for me? I would greatly appreciate it. I am available most mornings, if that's convenient for you.

It very well may happen that your employer contact wishes you to communicate by e-mail. The infomercial quoted above could easily be rewritten for an e-mail message. You should "cut and paste" your résumé right into the e-mail text itself.

Other effective self-promotion tools include portfolios for those in the arts, writing professions, or teaching. Portfolios show examples of work, photographs of projects or classroom activities, or certificates and credentials that are job related. There may not be an opportunity to use the portfolio during an interview, and it is not something that should be left with the organization. It is designed to be explained and displayed by the creator. However, during some networking meetings, there may be an opportunity to illustrate a point or strengthen a qualification by exhibiting the portfolio.

Beginning the Networking Process

Set the Tone for Your Communications

It can be useful to establish "tone words" for any communications you embark upon. Before making your first telephone call or writing your first letter, decide what you want the person to think of you. If you are networking to try to obtain a job, your tone words might include descriptors such as *genuine, informed,* and *self-knowledgeable.* When you're trying to acquire information, your tone words may have a slightly different focus, such as *courteous, organized, focused,* and *well-spoken.* Use the tone words you establish for your contacts to guide you through the networking process.

Honestly Express Your Intentions

When contacting individuals, it is important to be honest about your reasons for making the contact. Establish your purpose in your own mind and be able and ready to articulate it concisely. Determine an initial agenda, whether it be informational questioning or self-promotion, present it to your contact, and be ready to respond immediately. If you don't adequately prepare before initiating your overture, you may find yourself at a disadvantage if you're asked to immediately begin your informational interview or self-promotion during the first phone conversation or visit.

Start Networking Within Your Circle of Confidence

Once you have organized your approach—by utilizing specific researching methods, creating a system for keeping track of the people you will contact, and developing effective self-promotion tools—you are ready to begin networking. The best way to begin networking is by talking with a group of people you trust and feel comfortable with. This group is usually made up of your family, friends, and career counselors. No matter who is in this inner circle, they will have a special interest in seeing you succeed in your job search. In addition, because they will be easy to talk to, you should try taking some risks in terms of practicing your information-seeking approach. Gain confidence in talking about the strengths you bring to an organization and the underdeveloped skills you feel hinder your candidacy. Be sure to review the section on self-assessment for tips on approaching each of these areas. Ask for critical but constructive feedback from the people in your circle of confidence on the letters you write and the one-minute infomercial you have developed. Evaluate whether you want to make the changes they suggest, then practice the changes on others within this circle.

Stretch the Boundaries of Your Networking Circle of Confidence

Once you have refined the promotional tools you will use to accomplish your networking goals, you will want to make additional contacts. Because you will not know most of these people, it will be a less comfortable activity to undertake. The practice that you gained with your inner circle of trusted friends should have prepared you to now move outside of that comfort zone.

It is said that any information a person needs is only two phone calls away, but the information cannot be gained until you (1) make a reasonable guess about who might have the information you need and (2) pick up the telephone to make the call. Using your network list that includes alumni, instructors, supervisors, employers, and associations, you can begin preparing your list of questions that will allow you to get the information you need.

Prepare the Questions You Want to Ask

Networkers can provide you with the insider's perspective on any given field and you can ask them questions that you might not want to ask in an interview. For example, you can ask them to describe the more repetitious or mundane parts of the job or ask them for a realistic idea of salary expectations. Be sure to prepare your questions ahead of time so that you are organized and efficient.

Be Prepared to Answer Some Questions

To communicate effectively, you must anticipate questions that will be asked of you by the networkers you contact. Revisit the self-assessment process you undertook and the research you've done so that you can effortlessly respond to questions about your short- and long-term goals and the kinds of jobs you are most interested in pursuing.

General Networking Tips

Make Every Contact Count. Setting the tone for each interaction is critical. Approaches that will help you communicate in an effective way include politeness, being appreciative of time provided to you, and being prepared and thorough. Remember, *everyone* within an organization has a circle of influence, so be prepared to interact effectively with each person you encounter in the networking process, including secretarial and support staff. Many information or job seekers have thwarted their own efforts by being rude to some individuals they encountered as they networked because they made the incorrect assumption that certain persons were unimportant.

Sometimes your contacts may be surprised at their ability to help you. After meeting and talking with you, they might think they have not offered much in the way of help. A day or two later, however, they may make a contact that would be useful to you and refer you to that person.

With Each Contact, Widen Your Circle of Networkers. Always leave an informational interview with the names of at least two more people who can help you get the information or job that you are seeking. Don't be shy about asking for additional contacts; networking is all about increasing the number of people you can interact with to achieve your goals.

Make Your Own Decisions. As you talk with different people and get answers to the questions you pose, you may hear conflicting information or get conflicting suggestions. Your job is to listen to these "experts" and decide what information and which suggestions will help you achieve *your* goals. Only implement those suggestions that you believe will work for you.

Shutting Down Your Network

As you achieve the goals that motivated your networking activity—getting the information you need or the job you want—the time will come to inactivate all or parts of your network. As you do, be sure to tell your primary supporters about your change in status. Call or write to each one of them and give them as many details about your new status as you feel is necessary to maintain a positive relationship.

Because a network takes on a life of its own, activity undertaken on your behalf will continue even after you cease your efforts. As you get calls or are contacted in some fashion, be sure to inform these networkers about your change in status, and thank them for assistance they have provided.

Information on the latest employment trends indicates that workers will change jobs or careers several times in their lifetime. Networking, then, will be a critical aspect in the span of your professional life. If you carefully and thoughtfully conduct your networking activities during your job search, you will have a solid foundation of experience when you need to network the next time around.

Where Are These Jobs, Anyway?

Having a list of job titles that you've designed around your own career interests and skills is an excellent beginning. It means you've really thought about who you are and what you are presenting to the employment market. It has caused you to think seriously about the most appealing environments to work in, and you have identified some employer types that represent these environments.

The research and the thinking that you've done thus far will be used again and again. They will be helpful in writing your résumé and cover letters, in talking about yourself on the telephone to prospective employers, and in answering interview questions.

Now is a good time to begin to narrow the field of job titles and employment sites down to some specific employers to initiate the employment contact.

Find Out Which Employers Hire People Like You

This section will provide tips, techniques, and specific resources for developing an actual list of specific employers that can be used to make contacts. It is only an outline that you must be prepared to tailor to your own particular needs and according to what you bring to the job search. Once again, it is important to communicate with others along the way exactly what you're looking for and what your goals are for the research you're doing. Librarians, employers, career counselors, friends, friends of friends, business contacts, and bookstore staff will all have helpful information on geographically specific and new resources to aid you in locating employers who'll hire you.

Identify Information Resources

Your interview wardrobe and your new résumé might have put a dent in your wallet, but the resources you'll need to pursue your job search are available for free. The categories of information detailed here are not hard to find and are yours for the browsing.

Numerous resources described in this section will help you identify actual employers. Use all of them or any others that you identify as available in your geographic area. As you become experienced in this process, you'll quickly figure out which information sources are helpful and which are not. If you live in a rural area, a well-planned day trip to a major city that includes a college career office, a large college or city library, state and federal employment centers, a chamber of commerce office, and a well-stocked bookstore can produce valuable results.

There are many excellent resources available to help you identify actual job sites. They are categorized into employer directories (usually indexed by product lines and geographic location), geographically based directories (designed to highlight particular cities, regions, or states), career-specific directories (e.g., *Sports MarketPlace*, which lists tens of thousands of firms involved with sports), periodicals and newspapers, targeted job posting publications, and videos. This is by no means meant to be a complete treatment of resources but rather a starting point for identifying useful resources.

Working from the more general references to highly specific resources, we provide a basic list to help you begin your search. Many of these you'll find easily available. In some cases reference librarians and others will suggest even better materials for your particular situation. Start to create your own customized bibliography of job search references.

Geographically Based Directories. The Job Bank series published by Bob Adams, Inc. (aip.com) contains detailed entries on each area's major employers, including business activity, address, phone number, and hiring contact name. Many listings specify educational backgrounds being sought in potential employees. Each volume contains a solid discussion of each city's or state's major employment sectors. Organizations are also indexed by industry. Job

Bank volumes are available for the following places: Atlanta; Boston; Chicago; Dallas–Ft. Worth; Denver; Detroit; Florida; Houston; Los Angeles; Minneapolis; New York; Ohio; Philadelphia; San Francisco; Seattle; St. Louis; Washington, D.C.; and other cities throughout the Northwest.

National Job Bank (careercity.com) lists employers in every state, along with contact names and commonly hired job categories. Included are many small companies often overlooked by other directories. Companies are also indexed by industry. This publication provides information on educational backgrounds sought and lists company benefits.

Periodicals and Newspapers. Several sources are available to help you locate which journals or magazines carry job advertisements in your field. Other resources help you identify opportunities in other parts of the country.

- *Where the Jobs Are: A Comprehensive Directory of 1,200 Journals Listing Career Opportunities*
- *Corptech Fast 5,000 Company Locator*
- *National Ad Search* (nationaladsearch.com)
- *The Federal Jobs Digest* (jobsfed.com) and *Federal Career Opportunities*
- *World Chamber of Commerce Directory* (chamberofcommerce.org)

This list is certainly not exhaustive; use it to begin your job search work.

Targeted Job Posting Publications. Although the resources that follow are national in scope, they are either targeted to one medium of contact (telephone), focused on specific types of jobs, or less comprehensive than the sources previously listed.

- Careers.org (careers.org/index.html)
- *The Job Hunter* (jobhunter.com)
- *Current Jobs for Graduates* (graduatejobs.com)
- *Environmental Opportunities* (ecojobs.com)
- *Y National Vacancy List* (ymca.net/employment/ymca_recruiting/ jobright.htm)
- *ArtSEARCH*
- *Community Jobs*
- *National Association of Colleges and Employers: Job Choices series*
- *National Association of Colleges and Employers* (jobweb.com)

Videos. You may be one of the many job seekers who likes to get information via a medium other than paper. Many career libraries, public libraries, and career centers in libraries carry an assortment of videos that will help you learn new techniques and get information helpful in the job search.

Locate Information Resources

Throughout these introductory chapters, we have continually referred you to various websites for information on everything from job listings to career information. Using the Web gives you a mobility at your computer that you don't enjoy if you rely solely on books or newspapers or printed journals. Moreover, material on the Web, if the site is maintained, can be the most up-to-date information available.

You'll eventually identify the information resources that work best for you, but make certain you've covered the full range of resources before you begin to rely on a smaller list. Here's a short list of informational sites that many job seekers find helpful:

- Public and college libraries
- College career centers
- Bookstores
- The Internet
- Local and state government personnel offices
- Career/job fairs

Each one of these sites offers a collection of resources that will help you get the information you need.

As you meet and talk with service professionals at all these sites, be sure to let them know what you're doing. Inform them of your job search, what you've already accomplished, and what you're looking for. The more people who know you're job seeking, the greater the possibility that someone will have information or know someone who can help you along your way.

4

Interviewing and Job Offer Considerations

Certainly, there can be no one part of the job search process more fraught with anxiety and worry than the interview. Yet seasoned job seekers welcome the interview and will often say, "Just get me an interview and I'm on my way!" They understand that the interview is crucial to the hiring process and equally crucial for them, as job candidates, to have the opportunity of a personal dialogue to add to what the employer may already have learned from the résumé, cover letter, and telephone conversations.

Believe it or not, the interview is to be welcomed, and even enjoyed! It is a perfect opportunity for you, the candidate, to sit down with an employer and express yourself and display who you are and what you want. Of course, it takes thought and planning and a little strategy; after all, it *is* a job interview! But it can be a positive, if not pleasant, experience and one you can look back on and feel confident about your performance and effort.

For many new job seekers, a job, any job, seems a wonderful thing. But seasoned interview veterans know that the job interview is an important step for both sides—the employer and the candidate—to see what each has to offer and whether there is going to be a "fit" of personalities, work styles, and attitudes. And it is this concept of balance in the interview, that both sides have important parts to play, that holds the key to success in mastering this aspect of the job search strategy.

Try to think of the interview as a conversation between two interested and equal partners. You both have important, even vital, information to deliver and to learn. Of course, there's no denying the employer has some leverage, especially in the initial interview for recruitment or any interview scheduled by the candidate and not the recruiter. That should not prevent the interviewee from seeking to play an equal part in what should be a fair exchange of information. Too often the untutored candidate allows the interview to become one-sided. The employer asks all the questions and the candidate simply responds. The ideal would be for two mutually interested parties to sit down and discuss possibilities for each. This is a conversation of significance, and it requires preparation, thought about the tone of the interview, and planning of the nature and details of the information to be exchanged.

Preparing for the Interview

The length of most initial interviews is about thirty minutes. Given the brevity, the information that is exchanged ought to be important. The candidate should be delivering material that the employer cannot discover on the résumé, and in turn, the candidate should be learning things about the employer that he or she could not otherwise find out. After all, if you have only thirty minutes, why waste time on information that is already published? The information exchanged is more than just factual, and both sides will learn much from what they see of each other, as well. How the candidate looks, speaks, and acts are important to the employer. The employer's attention to the interview and awareness of the candidate's résumé, the setting, and the quality of information presented are important to the candidate.

Just as the employer has every right to be disappointed when a prospect is late for the interview, looks unkempt, and seems ill-prepared to answer fairly standard questions, the candidate may be disappointed with an interviewer who isn't ready for the meeting, hasn't learned the basic résumé facts, and is constantly interrupted by telephone calls. In either situation there's good reason to feel let down.

There are many elements to a successful interview, and some of them are not easy to describe or prepare for. Sometimes there is just a chemistry between interviewer and interviewee that brings out the best in both, and a good exchange takes place. But there is much the candidate can do to pave the way for success in terms of his or her résumé, personal appearance, goals, and interview strategy—each of which we will discuss. However, none of this preparation is as important as the time and thought the candidate gives to personal self-assessment.

Self-Assessment
Neither a stunning résumé nor an expensive, well-tailored suit can compensate for candidates who do not know what they want, where they are going, or why they are interviewing with a particular employer. Self-assessment, the

process by which we begin to know and acknowledge our own particular blend of education, experiences, needs, and goals, is not something that can be sorted out the weekend before a major interview. Of all the elements of interview preparation, this one requires the longest lead time and cannot be faked.

Because the time allotted for most interviews is brief, it is all the more important for job candidates to understand and express succinctly why they are there and what they have to offer. This is not a time for undue modesty (or for braggadocio either); it is a time for a compelling, reasoned statement of why you feel that you and this employer might make a good match. It means you have to have thought about your skills, interests, and attributes; related those to your life experiences and your own history of challenges and opportunities; and determined what that indicates about your strengths, preferences, values, and areas needing further development.

If you need some assistance with self-assessment issues, refer to Chapter 1. Included are suggested exercises that can be done as needed, such as making up an experiential diary and extracting obvious strengths and weaknesses from past experiences. These simple assignments will help you look at past activities as collections of tasks with accompanying skills and responsibilities. Don't overlook your high school or college career office. Many offer personal counseling on self-assessment issues and may provide testing instruments such as the *Myers-Briggs Type Indicator (MBTI)*, the *Harrington-O'Shea Career Decision-Making System (CDM)*, the *Strong Interest Inventory (SII)*, or any other of a wide selection of assessment tools that can help you clarify some of these issues prior to the interview stage of your job search.

The Résumé

Résumé preparation has been discussed in detail, and some basic examples were provided. In this section we want to concentrate on how best to use your résumé in the interview. In most cases the employer will have seen the résumé prior to the interview, and, in fact, it may well have been the quality of that résumé that secured the interview opportunity.

An interview is a conversation, however, and not an exercise in reading. So, if the employer hasn't seen your résumé and you have brought it along to the interview, wait until asked or until the end of the interview to offer it. Otherwise, you may find yourself staring at the back of your résumé and simply answering "yes" and "no" to a series of questions drawn from that document.

Sometimes an interviewer is not prepared and does not know or recall the contents of the résumé and may use the résumé to a greater or lesser degree as a "prompt" during the interview. It is for you to judge what that may indicate about the individual performing the interview or the employer. If your interviewer seems surprised by the scheduled meeting, relies on the résumé to an inordinate degree, and seems otherwise unfamiliar with your background, this lack of preparation for the hiring process could well be a symptom of general management disorganization or may simply be the result of poor planning on the part of one individual. It is your responsibility as a potential employee to be aware of these signals and make your decisions accordingly.

It is perfectly acceptable for you to guide the conversation if you feel that it is quickly becoming directionless and not conducive to best highlighting your skills and talents. You may say something like, "Mr. Smith, you might be interested in some recent interpreting experience I gained in a volunteer position at our local hospital that is not detailed on my résumé. May I tell you about it?" This can return the interview to two people talking to each other, not one reading and the other responding.

By all means, bring at least one copy of your résumé to the interview. Occasionally, at the close of an interview, an interviewer will express an interest in circulating a résumé to several departments, and you could then offer the copy you brought. Sometimes, an interview appointment provides an opportunity to meet others in the organization who may express an interest in you and your background, and it may be helpful to follow up with a copy of your résumé. Our best advice, however, is to keep it out of sight until needed or requested.

Employer Information

Whether your interview is for graduate school admission, an overseas corporate position, or a position with a local company, it is important to know something about the employer or the organization. Keeping in mind that the interview is relatively brief and that you will hopefully have other interviews with other organizations, it is important to keep your research in proportion. If secondary interviews are called for, you will have additional time to do further research. For the first interview, it is helpful to know the organization's mission, goals, size, scope of operations, and so forth. Your research may uncover recent areas of challenge or particular successes that may help to fuel the interview. Use the "What Do They Call the Job You Want?" section of Chapter 3, your library, and your career or guidance office to help you locate this information in the most efficient way possible. Don't be shy in asking advice of these counseling and guidance professionals on how best to spend your preparation time. With some practice, you'll soon learn how much information is enough and which kinds of information are most useful to you.

Interview Content

We've already discussed how it can help to think of the interview as an important conversation—one that, as with any conversation, you want to find pleasant and interesting and to leave you with a good feeling. But because this conversation is especially important, the information that's exchanged is critical to its success. What do you want them to know about you? What do you need to know about them? What interview technique do you need to particularly pay attention to? How do you want to manage the close of the interview? What steps will follow in the hiring process?

Except for the professional interviewer, most of us find interviewing stressful and anxiety-provoking. Developing a strategy before you begin interviewing will help you relieve some stress and anxiety. One particular strategy that has worked for many and may work for you is interviewing by objective. Before you interview, write down three to five goals you would like to achieve for that interview. They may be technique goals: smile a little more, have a firmer handshake, be sure to ask about the next stage in the interview process before leaving. They may be content-oriented goals: find out about the company's current challenges and opportunities; be sure to speak of your recent research, writing experiences, or foreign travel. Whatever your goals, jot down a few of them as goals for each interview.

Most people find that in trying to achieve these few goals, their interviewing technique becomes more organized and focused. After the interview, the most common question friends and family ask is "How did it go?" With this technique, you have an indication of whether you met *your* goals for the meeting, not just some vague idea of how it went. Chances are, if you accomplished what you wanted to, it improved the quality of the entire interview. As you continue to interview, you will want to revise your goals to continue improving your interview skills.

Now, add to the concept of the significant conversation the idea of a beginning, a middle, and a closing and you will have two thoughts that will give your interview a distinctive character. Be sure to make your introduction warm and cordial. Say your full name (and if it's a difficult-to-pronounce name, help the interviewer to pronounce it) and make certain you know your interviewer's name and how to pronounce it. Most interviews begin with some "soft talk" about the weather, chat about the candidate's trip to the interview site, or national events. This is done as a courtesy to relax both you and the interviewer, to get you talking, and to generally try to defuse the atmosphere of excessive tension. Try to be yourself, engage in the conversation, and don't try to second-guess the interviewer. This is simply what it appears to be—casual conversation.

Once you and the interviewer move on to exchange more serious information in the middle part of the interview, the two most important concerns become your ability to handle challenging questions and your success at asking meaningful ones. Interviewer questions will probably fall into one of three categories: personal assessment and career direction, academic assessment, and knowledge of the employer. Here are a few examples of questions in each category:

Personal Assessment and Career Direction
1. What motivates you to put forth your best effort?
2. What do you consider to be your greatest strengths and weaknesses?
3. What qualifications do you have that make you think you will be successful in this career?

Academic Assessment
1. What led you to choose your major?
2. What subjects did you like best and least? Why?
3. How has your college experience prepared you for this career?

Knowledge of the Employer
1. What do you think it takes to be successful in an organization like ours?
2. In what ways do you think you can make a contribution to our organization?
3. Why did you choose to seek a position with this organization?

The interviewer wants a response to each question but is also gauging your enthusiasm, preparedness, and willingness to communicate. In each response you should provide some information about yourself that can be related to the employer's needs. A common mistake is to give too much information. Answer each question completely, but be careful not to run on too long with extensive details or examples.

Questions About Underdeveloped Skills

Most employers interview people who have met some minimum criteria of education and experience. They interview candidates to see who they are, to learn what kind of personality they exhibit, and to get some sense of how they might fit into the existing organization. It may be that you are asked about skills the employer hopes to find and that you have not documented. Maybe it's grant-writing experience, knowledge of the European political system, or a knowledge of the film world.

To questions about skills and experiences you don't have, answer honestly and forthrightly and try to offer some additional information about skills you do have. For example, perhaps the employer is disappointed you have no grant-writing experience. An honest answer may be as follows:

> *No, unfortunately, I was never in a position to acquire those skills. I do understand something of the complexities of the grant-writing process and feel confident that my attention to detail, careful reading skills, and strong writing would make grants a wonderful challenge in a new job. I think I could get up on the learning curve quickly.*

The employer hears an honest admission of lack of experience but is reassured by some specific skill details that do relate to grant writing and a confident manner that suggests enthusiasm and interest in a challenge.

For many students, questions about their possible contribution to an employer's organization can prove challenging. Because your education has probably not included specific training for a job, you need to review your academic record and select capabilities you have developed in your major that an employer can appreciate. For example, perhaps you read well and can analyze and condense what you've read into smaller, more focused pieces. That could be valuable. Or maybe you did some serious research and you know you have valuable investigative skills. Your public speaking might be highly developed and you might use visual aids appropriately and effectively. Or maybe your skill at correspondence, memos, and messages is effective. Whatever it is, you must take it out of the academic context and put it into a new, employer-friendly context so your interviewer can best judge how you could help the organization.

Exhibiting knowledge of the organization will, without a doubt, show the interviewer that you are interested enough in the available position to have done some legwork in preparation for the interview. Remember, it is not necessary to know every detail of the organization's history but rather to have a general knowledge about why it is in business and how the industry is faring.

Sometime during the interview, generally after the midway point, you'll be asked if you have any questions for the interviewer. Your questions will tell the employer much about your attitude and your desire to understand the organization's expectations so you can compare them to your own strengths. The following are just a few questions you might want to ask:

1. What is the communication style of the organization? (meetings, memos, and so forth)
2. What would a typical day in this position be like for me?
3. What have been some of the interesting challenges and opportunities your organization has recently faced?

Most interviews draw to a natural closing point, so be careful not to prolong the discussion. At a signal from the interviewer, wind up your presentation, express your appreciation for the opportunity, and be sure to ask what the next stage in the process will be. When can you expect to hear from them? Will they be conducting second-tier interviews? If you are interested and haven't heard, would they mind a phone call? Be sure to collect a business card with the name and phone number of your interviewer. On your way out, you might have an opportunity to pick up organizational literature you haven't seen before.

With the right preparation—a thorough self-assessment, professional clothing, and employer information—you'll be able to set and achieve the goals you have established for the interview process.

Interview Follow-Up

Quite often there is a considerable time lag between interviewing for a position and being hired or, in the case of the networker, between your phone call or letter to a possible contact and the opportunity of a meeting. This can be frustrating. "Why aren't they contacting me?" "I thought I'd get another interview, but no one has telephoned." "Am I out of the running?" You don't know what is happening.

Consider the Differing Perspectives

Of course, there is another perspective that of the networker or hiring organization. Organizations are complex, with multiple tasks that need to be accomplished each day. Hiring is a discrete activity that does not occur as frequently as other job assignments. The hiring process might have to take second place to other, more immediate organizational needs. Although it may be very important to you, and it is certainly ultimately significant to the employer, other issues such as fiscal management, planning and product development, employer vacation periods, or financial constraints may prevent an organization or individual within that organization from acting on your employment or your request for information as quickly as you or they would prefer.

Use Your Communication Skills

Good communication is essential here to resolve any anxieties, and the responsibility is on you, the job or information seeker. Too many job seekers and networkers offer as an excuse that they don't want to "bother" the organization by writing letters or calling. Let us assure you here and now that if you are troubling an organization by over-communicating, someone will indicate that situation to you quite clearly. If not, you can only assume you are a worthwhile prospect and the employer appreciates being reminded of your availability and interest. Let's look at follow-up practices in the job interview process and the networking situation separately.

Following Up on the Employment Interview

A brief thank-you note following an interview is an excellent and polite way to begin a series of follow-up communications with a potential employer with whom you have interviewed and want to remain in touch. It should be just that—a thank-you for a good meeting. If you failed to mention some fact or experience during your interview that you think might add to your candidacy, you may use this note to do that. However, this should be essentially a note whose overall tone is appreciative and, if appropriate, indicative of a continuing interest in pursuing any opportunity that may exist with that organization. It is one of the few pieces of business correspondence that may be handwritten, but always use plain, good-quality, standard-size paper.

If, however, at this point you are no longer interested in the employer, the thank-you note is an appropriate time to indicate that. You are under no obligation to identify any reason for not continuing to pursue employment with that organization, but if you are so inclined to indicate your professional reasons (pursuing other employers more akin to your interests, looking for greater income production than this employer can provide, a different geographic location), you certainly may. It should not be written with an eye to negotiation, for it will not be interpreted as such.

As part of your interview closing, you should have taken the initiative to establish lines of communication for continuing information about your candidacy. If you asked permission to telephone, wait a week following your thank-you note, then telephone your contact simply to inquire how things are progressing on your employment status. The feedback you receive here should be taken at face value. If your interviewer simply has no information, he or she will tell you so and indicate whether you should call again and when. Don't be discouraged if this should continue over some period of time.

If during this time something occurs that you think improves or changes your candidacy (some new qualification or experience you may have had), including any offers from other organizations, by all means telephone or write to inform the employer about this. In the case of an offer from a competing but less desirable or equally desirable organization, telephone your contact, explain what has happened, express your real interest in the organization, and inquire whether some determination on your employment might be made before you must respond to this other offer. An organization that is truly interested in you may be moved to make a decision about your candidacy. Equally possible is the scenario in which they are not yet ready to make a decision and so advise you to take the offer that has been presented. Again, you have no ethical alternative but to deal with the information presented in a straightforward manner.

When accepting other employment, be sure to contact any employers still actively considering you and inform them of your new job. Thank them graciously for their consideration. There are many other job seekers out there just like you who will benefit from having their candidacy improved when others bow out of the race. Who knows, you might at some future time have occasion to interact professionally with one of the organizations with which you sought employment. How embarrassing it would be to have someone remember you as the candidate who failed to notify them that you were taking a job elsewhere!

In all of your follow-up communications, keep good notes of whom you spoke with, when you called, and any instructions that were given about return communications. This will prevent any misunderstandings and provide you with good records of what has transpired.

Job Offer Considerations

For many recent college graduates, the thrill of their first job and, for some, the most substantial regular income they have ever earned seems an excess of good fortune coming at once. To question that first income or to be critical in any way of the conditions of employment at the time of the initial offer seems like looking a gift horse in the mouth. It doesn't seem to occur to many new hires even to attempt to negotiate any aspect of their first job. And, as many employers who deal with entry-level jobs for recent college graduates will readily confirm, the reality is that there simply isn't much movement in salary available to these new college recruits. The entry-level hire generally does not have an employment track record on a professional level to provide any leverage for negotiation. Real negotiations on salary, benefits, retirement provisions, and so forth come to those with significant employment records at higher income levels.

Of course, the job offer is more than just money. It can be composed of geographic assignment, duties and responsibilities, training, benefits, health and medical insurance, educational assistance, car allowance or company vehicle, and a host of other items. All of this is generally detailed in the formal letter that presents the final job offer. In most cases this is a follow-up to a personal phone call from the employer representative who has been principally responsible for your hiring process.

That initial telephone offer is certainly binding as a verbal agreement, but most firms follow up with a detailed letter outlining the most significant parts of your employment contract. You may, of course, choose to respond immediately at the time of the telephone offer (which would be considered a binding oral contract), but you will also be required to formally answer the letter of offer with a letter of acceptance, restating the salient elements of the employer's description of your position, salary, and benefits. This ensures that both parties are clear on the terms and conditions of employment and remuneration and any other outstanding aspects of the job offer.

Is This the Job You Want?

Most new employees will respond affirmatively in writing, glad to be in the position to accept employment. If you've worked hard to get the offer and the job market is tight, other offers may not be in sight, so you will say, "Yes, I accept!" What is important here is that the job offer you accept be one that does fit your particular needs, values, and interests as you've outlined them in your self-assessment process. Moreover, it should be a job that will not only use your skills and education but also challenge you to develop new skills and talents.

Jobs are sometimes accepted too hastily, for the wrong reasons, and without proper scrutiny by the applicant. For example, an individual might readily accept a sales job only to find the continual rejection by potential clients unendurable. An office worker might realize within weeks the constraints of a desk job and yearn for more activity. Employment is an important part of our lives. It is, for most of our adult lives, our most continuous productive activity. We want to make good choices based on the right criteria.

If you have a low tolerance for risk, a job based on commission will certainly be very anxiety-provoking. If being near your family is important, issues of relocation could present a decision crisis for you. If you're an adventurous person, a job with frequent travel would provide needed excitement and be very desirable. The importance of income, the need to continue your education, your personal health situation—all of these have an impact on whether the job you are considering will ultimately meet your needs. Unless you've spent some time understanding and thinking about these issues, it will be difficult to evaluate offers you do receive.

More important, if you make a decision that you cannot tolerate and feel you must leave that job, you will then have both unemployment and self-esteem issues to contend with. These will combine to make the next job search tough going, indeed. So make your acceptance a carefully considered decision.

Negotiate Your Offer

It may be that there is some aspect of your job offer that is not particularly attractive to you. Perhaps there is no relocation allotment to help you move your possessions, and this presents some financial hardship for you. It may be that the health insurance is less than you had hoped. Your initial assignment may be different from what you expected, either in its location or in the duties and responsibilities that comprise it. Or it may simply be that the salary is less than you anticipated. Other considerations may be your official starting date of employment, vacation time, evening hours, dates of training programs or schools, and other concerns.

If you are considering not accepting the job because of some item or items in the job offer "package" that do not meet your needs, you should know that most employers emphatically wish that you would bring that issue to their attention. It may be that the employer can alter it to make the offer more agreeable for you. In some cases it cannot be changed. In any event the employer would generally like to have the opportunity to try to remedy a difficulty rather than risk losing a good potential employee over an issue that might have been resolved. After all, they have spent time and funds in securing your services, and they certainly deserve an opportunity to resolve any possible differences.

Honesty is the best approach in discussing any objections or uneasiness you might have over the employer's offer. Having received your formal offer in writing, contact your employer representative and indicate your particular dissatisfaction in a straightforward manner. For example, you might explain that while you are very interested in being employed by this organization, the salary (or any other benefit) is less than you have determined you require. State the terms you need, and listen to the response. You may be asked to put this in writing, or you may be asked to hold off until the firm can decide on a response. If you are dealing with a senior representative of the organization, one who has been involved in hiring for some time, you may get an immediate response or a solid indication of possible outcomes.

Perhaps the issue is one of relocation. Your initial assignment is in the Midwest, and because you had indicated a strong West Coast preference, you are surprised at the actual assignment. You might simply indicate that while you understand the need for the company to assign you based on its needs, you are disappointed and had hoped to be placed on the West Coast. You could inquire if that were still possible and, if not, would it be reasonable to expect a West Coast relocation in the future.

If your request is presented in a reasonable way, most employers will not see this as jeopardizing your offer. If they can agree to your proposal, they will. If not, they will simply tell you so, and you may choose to continue your candidacy with them or remove yourself from consideration. The choice will be up to you.

Some firms will adjust benefits within their parameters to meet the candidate's need if at all possible. If a candidate requires a relocation cost allowance, he or she may be asked to forgo tuition benefits for the first year to accomplish this adjustment. An increase in life insurance may be adjusted by some other benefit trade-off; perhaps a family dental plan is not needed. In these decisions you are called upon, sometimes under time pressure, to know how you value these issues and how important each is to you.

Many employers find they are more comfortable negotiating for candidates who have unique qualifications or who bring especially needed expertise to the organization. Employers hiring large numbers of entry-level college graduates may be far more reluctant to accommodate any changes in offer conditions. They are well supplied with candidates with similar education and experience so that if rejected by one candidate, they can draw new candidates from an ample labor pool.

Compare Offers

The condition of the economy, the job seeker's academic major and particular geographic job market, and individual needs and demands for certain employment conditions may not provide more than one job offer at a time. Some job seekers may feel that no reasonable offer should go unaccepted for the simple fear there won't be another.

In a tough job market, or if the job you seek is not widely available, or when your job search goes on too long and becomes difficult to sustain financially and emotionally, it may be necessary to accept an inferior offer. The alternative is continued unemployment. Even here, when you feel you don't have a choice, you can at least understand that in accepting this particular offer, there may be limitations and conditions you don't appreciate. At the time of acceptance, there were no other alternatives, but you can begin to use that position to gain the experience and talent to move toward a more attractive position.

Sometimes, however, more than one offer is received, and the candidate has the luxury of choice. If the job seeker knows what he or she wants and has done the necessary self-assessment honestly and thoroughly, it may be clear that one of the offers conforms more closely to those expressed wants and needs.

However, if, as so often happens, the offers are similar in terms of conditions and salary, the question then becomes which organization might provide the necessary climate, opportunities, and advantages for your professional development and growth. This is the time when solid employer research and astute questioning during the interviews really pay off. How much did you learn about the employer through your own research and skillful questioning? When the interviewer asked during the interview "Do you have any questions?" did you ask the kinds of questions that would help resolve a choice between one organization and another? Just as an employer must decide among numerous applicants, so must the applicant learn to assess the potential employer. Both are partners in the job search.

Reneging on an Offer

An especially disturbing occurrence for employers and career counseling professionals is when a job seeker formally (either orally or by written contract) accepts employment with one organization and later reneges on the agreement and goes with another employer.

There are all kinds of rationalizations offered for this unethical behavior. None of them satisfies. The sad irony is that what the job seeker is willing to do to the employer—make a promise and then break it—he or she would be outraged to have done to him- or herself: have the job offer pulled. It is a very bad way to begin a career. It suggests the individual has not taken the time to do the necessary self-assessment and self-awareness exercises to think and judge critically. The new offer taken may, in fact, be no better or worse than the one refused. You should be aware that there have been incidents of legal action following job candidates' reneging on an offer. This adds a very sour note to what should be a harmonious beginning of a lifelong adventure.

PART TWO

THE CAREER PATHS

5

Introduction to the Foreign Language Career Paths

Foreign language study is wonderful preparation for any number of careers. With its emphasis on communication and skills in writing, speaking, reading, and simply making connections between people, knowledge of a foreign language is also an education in your own language. This knowledge will serve the graduate well in any sector of the employment market.

As you examine several career paths possible with a foreign language degree, keep in mind that these are only representative career paths and typical ones at that. A Spanish major can become an accountant, and someone with a graduate degree in Romance languages can manage an organization. An academic degree is only one small part of what we have to offer an employer; it represents a fraction of our interests and experience. We bring life experiences and our paid and unpaid work history as well as our academic degree to the employment market.

Prospective employers can make some assumptions about foreign language graduates: they are skilled communicators, and they are interested in other cultures. In addition, employers could logically assume that students of foreign language are flexible, open to change, and tolerant of diversity. Even without having met you, an employer reading your résumé and seeing your degree in a foreign language could easily make these assumptions about you as a person and a potential worker.

Are Language Skills Practical?

The practical applications of knowing another language are obvious: When you travel, your experiences, meetings with native speakers, and cultural understanding do not have to be filtered through the medium of translation.

Americans learning a language often say, "But what does this mean in English?" There are countless expressions, moods, idiomatic phrases, proverbs, and jokes in any language, however, that simply cannot be translated. One must appreciate them in their original languages. To translate them is to receive out-of-focus images of the original.

If you know a foreign language, you benefit by not having to resort to transcribing everything back into English. When traveling, you can avoid the cultural filtering process that results in relating everything new to something already within your cultural context. For many, a croissant becomes a "roll" or a "breakfast roll"—neither English translation even begins to approximate what is suggested by the French. And if we use the translation "crescent roll," which does suggest something of the French word, we unfortunately bring to mind an American product that couldn't be further in appearance or taste from the French original.

There are native speakers in every country who do not speak any English. Without knowledge of a foreign language, you cannot easily approach these individuals to hear their stories, their words. Using an intermediary to translate is a very different experience. It is a filtering process of another kind that leaves both parties wondering how their words have been translated and whether the meanings being conveyed are accurate. This certainly gets in the way of honest and direct communication.

Without knowledge of a foreign language, published materials in that language also remain inaccessible. The detail and information they provide may be translated superficially, but the original information in its completeness will be available only to those who know the language.

How Will You Use Your Language Skills?

Language can be used either as a primary or an auxiliary skill in a career. If a foreign language is a primary skill in your job, you are using the language every day; you could not do your job without your foreign language knowledge. If your language skill use is auxiliary, you are using other skills (e.g., managerial, accounting, writing, computer, media technology) alongside your language use, or your foreign language use on the job is intermittent.

After graduation, that first job or decision to attend graduate school will have much to do with whether you desire to place your language skills in a dominant or a peripheral role. If you decide you want to teach German at the college level, you will have to pursue a doctorate in German and will probably want to spend some extended time in German-speaking countries to improve your fluency and idiomatic grasp of the language, and to experience all of the cultural nuances available only to residents. Your language skill will be a primary and defining attribute in your job search.

If, on the other hand, you enjoy your German language skill but also want to try your hand in the business world, you may enter the job market with an organization that does business with companies in Germany. Even if most of the work is conducted in English, there will be ample opportunity to use your German. There will be fax transmissions, telephone calls, and pieces of correspondence in German that will require your expertise.

Or you might find an American firm operating in Germany that has both American and German employees and looks for an appreciation and understanding of both languages in each candidate considered for existing positions. In situations such as this, there will certainly be business visits back and forth for which your knowledge of both cultures could be invaluable. You might begin as an import/export expediter whose job is primarily administrative, but you will use your German language to help with correspondence and some telephone work. Knowledge of German isn't absolutely essential to the job, but it makes you more attractive to your employer.

Occasionally, students with language degrees are surprised and disappointed when business employers hire them on the basis of their language skills but do not necessarily rely on those talents once they are employed. An executive of a well-known pharmaceutical manufacturer stated the situation as follows:

Employees with foreign language skills are valued for their understanding of that culture and cultural nuances and their sensitivity to those. If we need translation, either simultaneously verbal or written, we can subcontract that work to specialists, but we need folks within our organization who understand and appreciate other cultures, and that is acquired through language training.

Where Else Can You Work?

A random search through the popular website careerbuilder.com using "foreign language" as a keyword search, presented several opportunities requiring primary or secondary use of a foreign language. Note the variety, location, emphasis, or lack of emphasis on language skills, breadth of employers (both private and governmental), and salaries, where indicated:

Education-Foreign Language Instructor. For students with severe emotional disabilities in a small residential school. Competitive salary scale and excellent benefits. Special Education certification with SED endorsement or Special Education approval preferred.

Project Manager-Foreign Language and Regional/Culture Expert. Foreign language, regional expertise and culture program manager for one of the following four regions: Middle East/North Africa, Asia/Pacific Rim, Eurasia/Sub-Saharan Africa or Central/South America. Support training management, knowledge management, and collection and analysis of training and operational data related to Navy-wide foreign language, regional expertise and culture programs in consonance with Chief of Naval Operations policies.

Intelligence Officers (Collection). Collect and provide intelligence to war fighters, defense-policy makers and force planners in the Department of Defense and the Intelligence Community. Serve in one of several functional areas, including Technology, Training, Evaluations, or Operations supporting senior managers and administrators. Orchestrate and interact with both technical and human resources to attain vital information and deduce the intentions of foreign governments and other nongovernmental organizations around the world. Salaries ranging from $77,353 to $139,774 depending upon a candidate's specific education and experience.

International Business Consultant. All levels for transfer pricing practice, in-depth analysis of client operation, advising clients, domestic/international manufacturing, R&D, marketing, and financial performance. Some travel is required. Bachelor's degree required and foreign language proficiency a plus.

Customer Service Representative. English speaking and bilingual (Spanish). Starting salary of $25,000 – $30,000. Primary telephone contact with customers and physicians for health insurance questions.

> **Medical Translator.** Translating various medical documents from English to Spanish and vice versa. Bachelor's degree in a health-related field. Management experience and work in premedicine, psychology, health-care admission preferred.

> **Editor.** Excellent communication skills, English/German or English/Italian preferred. Knowledge of MS Office and Internet usage. Edit foreign language instructionals for grade 5 through college.

Where Can Your Degree Take You?

Although we speak about careers we want to have, and there are career services offices on college campuses, the word "career" is best applied to a history of work. If you have a job in a retail establishment, you wouldn't be likely to call it a career. But if after ten years you are still working at the retail business in a managerial role, you could justifiably call that a career. In our lifetime progression from job to job, position to position, skill to skill, it is sometimes difficult to separate ourselves from our immediate concerns of job and home in order to view our life and our work from an objective, long-term perspective.

The idea of a career is best applied to a view of one's work over many years. Only then can we begin to see the interconnectedness of our work, which eludes us as we live it. If you ever have an opportunity to visit someone who has spent his or her life in a profession related to the use of another language, in a conversation on this topic you might witness that person's surprise at and new understanding of how many seemingly unrelated jobs that person held at various times that helped to build his or her current mastery of the profession.

In anticipating the transitions your career might make over the years, consider the possibility that the way you use your foreign language skills will change over time as well. The young government employee working for the Defense Intelligence Agency translating documents might one day become head of a large department and spend more time managing people than employing language skills, the very skills that gained the person his or her initial entry into the agency. On the other hand, a college librarian with a Japanese degree may find its usefulness increasing as the college receives growing numbers of Japanese students and the librarian finds it more helpful to communicate with these students in their native language.

Where Do You Begin Your Career Path Search?

In Chapters 6 through 10, we will examine several career paths, some of which require the use of a foreign language as a primary skill. These paths include the following:

1. Teaching
2. Translating and interpreting
3. Government
4. Educational administration
5. Business, industry, and commerce

In the cases of teaching and translating/interpreting, the primary focus of your job and career is facility with the language, both spoken and written. Your employment qualifications will center largely on your language skills. The other paths (government, educational administration, and business) comprise positions in which your foreign language may be used as an auxiliary skill. It may not be an essential requirement for the position, but it is certainly a welcome and useful adjunct to your other talents. The focus in these jobs is on a potential employee's skills package, which includes some degree of foreign language familiarity, but that has other qualifications to offer as well.

The career paths that follow are merely suggestions presented to stimulate your thinking about possible directions as you enter the workforce following graduation. Many travelers being on the same road, and entry-level jobs, even in different organizations, seem remarkably similar. Soon, however, the road divides, and we each begin to acquire different skills and experiences in our life's work. It is the acquisition of the skills package that often determines our career direction. The paths suggested are simply some of the many possible starting points.

Using Language as an Auxiliary Skill

As mentioned, Chapters 8 through 10 will cover career paths in government; educational administration; and business, industry, and commerce. These three chapters discuss options available to the foreign language major who chooses not to be hired primarily for his or her foreign language abilities. There are any number of reasons why you, as a graduate, seek such employment and why an employer seeking workers may consider education in a foreign language important to the career but not of prime significance.

One reason could be that your language skills are not sufficiently developed to stake your career on them. Perhaps you graduated with a degree in Russian language and literature. You had never studied Russian before college, and although you were a good student in college and have been to Russia once or twice, you simply are not fluent or confident enough in your command of Russian to seek a position that would depend on this talent.

Still, you love the Russian language and have enjoyed your exposure to the Russian culture. You hope to stay involved with that through your work, perhaps even finding a professional opportunity to visit Russia again. Your intentions might even include continuing to study the language. On the other hand, you have many other skills, talents, and interests that allow you to present yourself to an employer as someone other than a linguist. You might have substantial computer expertise, administrative ability, writing talent, or public presentation skills. Perhaps your quantitative abilities are strong, and you like working out problems with facts and numbers. Numerous opportunities are open to you that make use of these nonlanguage talents and your foreign language preparation.

On the employer's side, there may be reluctance to feature language skills as a requirement for employment and thus hire a new individual who may have only that talent. Most American organizations cannot afford to hire someone to work full-time solely on foreign language projects. In fact, when foreign language talent is a need, many business firms simply subcontract that work to local translators or interpreters. If those organizations send staff abroad, they will hire someone for the length of time required. No matter how expensive this kind of short-term service may be, it is far less expensive than employing someone year-round with a salary and benefits package. Some organizations have local employees abroad who are skilled in both their native tongue and English. An employer with European or Slavic subsidiaries might appreciate your language background and have every intention of using it occasionally, but the employer will also require other qualifications.

One persistent myth about putting your foreign language training to work for an American-based organization is that you will go to work immediately for some branch or subsidiary office based in the country whose language you speak. Nothing could be further from the truth. The reality is, in most cases, you cannot expect to be assigned overseas until you have mastered the corporate culture and climate of the employer. Foreign staffs are smaller and more exposed to the public and the press than are their domestic counterparts. It is essential that each employee sent overseas be thoroughly grounded in an understanding of and appreciation for the employing organization and its mission before representing it on foreign soil and this may take several years. Sometimes this means putting your use of the language on hold while you acquire other skills for the organization. You may be learning the product line for a consumer goods firm, acquiring detailed information about the manufacturing process in an industrial setting, or studying immigration and naturalization protocols as part of a position in collegiate student affairs. During your period of training in any job, you'll be learning about the competitive marketplace, accounting, computer systems, research, and any number of other business skills. Your employer may be well aware of your language background, so don't neglect it. Use any opportunities that present themselves at work to indicate your background and interests in that particular area of the world. When the call comes from your supervisor asking you to consider a foreign trip or assignment, he or she will expect your language skills to still be top-notch. Keep your skills fresh with an occasional evening course or self-directed learning program.

Another possible reason for not putting your language degree up front as a prime qualification for employment may have to do with how you see yourself. Perhaps in reviewing the exercises in the self-assessment chapter that opened this book, you realized there was much more to your aspirations and dreams about life after college than just using your academic major.

You may have new ideas now about what you want to do with your life. College has exposed you to other valuable skills. Maybe you realize you have good negotiation skills and you'd like to try those out in a career. College may have uncovered some creative abilities in art, theater, music, or dance that you were unaware of when you entered and now would like to continue to explore. Yet your degree and major may have remained constant. Nevertheless, you may want to try something new: sales, banking, theater administration, social work, or sports management. Not only is that reasonable, but you may also be surprised to find that your degree will not be undervalued.

And now—time to explore the career paths!

6

Path 1: Teaching

Perhaps the most familiar career path for people who want to use their foreign language education as a primary skill would be teaching. It is certainly the role model for employment that the student of foreign language has seen most often, and it may be that a particular teacher was the inspiration for a student's choice of this major in college.

It is certainly an attractive prospect to work with a body of information you love and to share that enjoyment with countless students over the years. There is learning for the instructor as well, which adds to the position's excitement. Most teachers readily admit they enjoy being students, and good teachers come to the classroom as ready to learn from students as students arrive hoping to learn from their teachers. Good teachers maintain a regular program of professional development, continuing to learn new classroom techniques and to improve their teaching methods.

Whether in grade school, high school, or at the university level, there is a fellowship and camaraderie among teachers. They share anecdotes about techniques that have or have not worked in the classroom. Many can also share an interest in the growth and development of particular students they pass along through the years. Students often come back and visit their formative teachers, which brings its own rewards to the teachers they visit.

For the foreign language teacher, there is another exciting dimension to what is taught. It is no hyperbole to say that the teacher of another language takes students on a magic carpet ride to a culture they usually know very little about. As students study a new culture, they begin to understand and become open to different ways of thinking, eating, living, believing, socializing, and celebrating. Foreign language teachers instill tolerance and an appreciation of the multiculturalism so evident in our lives today.

With the international nature of business, the ease and relatively low cost of foreign travel, and the increasing number of exchange programs, the field of teaching foreign language remains an attractive and viable alternative. Although English continues to be seen as the worldwide language of commerce, industry, and science, there is also a resurgence of traditionalism and a renewed awareness that to let a language die is to lose something irreplaceable.

We have seen this close to home in the Canadian province of Quebec, which has insisted on French as the language of culture, politics, commerce, and even tourism. Quebec remains a popular destination for English-speaking tourists who make every attempt to speak some French and who enjoy the province's focus on French as the primary language.

To the traditional career paths of high school, college, and professional language school venues, we can now add elementary schools in increasing numbers; these institutions continue to see growth in foreign language training for young children. Children in the elementary grades have little self-consciousness and are remarkable mimics. If foreign languages are introduced with a sense of fun and exuberance, these youngsters tend to absorb the material, setting the stage for a lifelong involvement with other languages, not to mention increasing the opportunities for prospective teachers.

The predictable result of an early school introduction to foreign language has been an extension of the foreign language curriculum in high schools to accommodate the proficiency of students arriving from the lower grades with four or even five years of previous language instruction. For the foreign language major in education, this sophistication is a pleasant surprise. It is attracting more and more foreign language teachers to the secondary level, where material that was once introduced at the college level is now taught. As these students graduate from high school and move on to college, we shall see similar growth in college language programs to provide challenges for this new generation of linguists. This is an exciting and encouraging trend.

Definition of the Career Path

Public and private schoolteachers can find a lifetime of career service in the classroom, exposing many thousands of students to their first foreign language experiences. Foreign language teaching might offer opportunities to travel abroad with students as well as to do collaborative work with theater, music, culinary arts, and other school departments. Administratively, the skilled senior teacher can become a department head and be a force for change in curriculum design, quality of instruction, and departmental management. Public schoolteacher contracts provide increasingly competitive salaries and benefits packages that include tuition reimbursement for additional education related to one's profession.

Teachers at the college level are afforded an opportunity to work with older and more committed students who may have already invested several years in studying a particular language. The work is more sophisticated, more challenging, and can go faster in the college curriculum. Often, too, colleges are well equipped with excellent language laboratories and library collections to support their departments so students can do serious exploration on any number of aspects of language and culture.

College student populations studying language tend to be larger, and consequently faculty size is greater than in public schools. Instead of two French faculty members in a high school, there may be four or five in a small public college and ten or more in a major university department. Many colleges have a general education curriculum that emphasizes the foreign language requirement. Demand has increased for foreign language courses, at least at the first- and second-year levels of the language as students meet these degree requirements.

The kind of collegiality fostered by a college foreign language department has its own attractions for some potential teachers. It can certainly result in an atmosphere more focused on the language and the teaching of that language than is possible in the public school environment, where ancillary duties, disciplinary problems, and shorter classes (and attention spans) can limit even the most dedicated teacher.

Foreign language teachers who opt for careers in professional language schools will enjoy meeting and teaching a never-ending stream of interesting students from all walks of life. Prospective tourists, businesspeople, missionaries, students, and lifelong learners will fill the language courses that are offered for a fee through commercial agencies. Many of these schools have superior reputations and provide total immersion techniques and high-quality materials to help learners master conversational aspects of a foreign language in a limited time. Some of the larger schools offer reading, writing, and cultural courses as well as language classes.

Different Teaching and Learning Styles

Teaching at any level—elementary, secondary, college, postgraduate, or in a professional language school—will provide its own unique rewards. Each setting also has its own employment conditions and hiring requirements, which will be discussed in the sections that follow. What is shared by all, however, is a love of the language being taught and an enthusiasm in sharing this language with others so that they, too, can master it. No foreign language exists isolated from its history, geography, art, politics, and economic setting, and the teacher of a language must enjoy this aspect of teaching as well. It is what keeps language vital. Students learn far more than a language; they learn about a culture, an ethos, and a way of life. Teachers must be prepared to share all of that with their students.

Baking French baguettes with students can be a point of departure not only for a discussion of French diet and eating patterns, but also for comparing the pace of life in various cultures. For a younger classroom of budding Francophiles, it might be enough to learn the French words *pain*, *croissant*, *buerre*, and *baguette* and to have fun baking and eating. For an older group, however, there are many other lessons in such an exercise: The French buy their bread every day. They buy it unwrapped and fresh from the oven, and they would never buy day-old bread for table use. These are quite different from mainstream American habits. One could discuss the implications of this behavior and the French views on packaging, marketing, and time available to buy groceries daily as well as French values that esteem small private bakers over large conglomerates.

It is far less unusual today than it was just a few years ago for French teachers in American schools to take students to France for a week or ten days. Well planned and designed to instill a true appreciation for everything French, these field trips can crystallize for many young students a love of language and appreciation for a culture different from their own. Some will go on to study French in college, and others will simply become better world citizens for the experience.

Learning a foreign language is sometimes spoken of as almost impossible to do. As a student of foreign language reading this book, you realize this is not so. It is like learning any new skill; it takes time, and, most of all, it takes practice. But to teach a foreign language well does require creativity, for people learn in different ways.

Your teaching-methods class in college will spend considerable time on the different teaching styles. You will identify your strengths as well as aspects of your basic style that may leave some students unsatisfied. You'll learn how to compensate for any shortcomings you may have in your teaching style. For a master's or doctorate degree, foreign language graduates who may not have the advantage of the formal teaching-methods preparation required in a teacher education program, will find the same information through conferences and professional associations of teachers of foreign language.

Students' learning styles vary. Some are visual learners. They enjoy board work, note taking, posters, signs, handouts, and drawings. They retain what they see and connect those memories by use of visual cues. The vocabulary of a barge trip down the Seine may be more easily remembered by watching a video than by listening to the teacher discuss or even pantomime the experience.

Some students have a strong response to auditory stimuli and enjoy hearing the language and listening to others speak it. They can easily mimic intonation and verbal phrasing. Auditory learners enjoy role-playing, theatrical pieces, watching films or videos of native speakers, and listening to a teacher who uses the language in class extensively. Language lab practice is also fun for these kinds of learners.

Movement, action, and participation characterize the learning style of kinesthetic learners. They need to be involved in role-playing, skits, and games to master the intricacies of a foreign language. Learning a Spanish dance helps to reinforce the words that go along with a piece of music. For these students, action is the key to learning.

This need to appeal to the kinesthetic, or action-oriented, learners has actually prompted an entire school of language teaching through the world-renowned efforts of a Dartmouth College French professor, John Arthur Rassias. The Rassias method of engaging students in the learning of language is taught in workshops and conferences all over the United States to help instructors appreciate the energy that can be created by a more interactive, dramatic classroom style. More important, Rassias has documented exponential jumps in learning using his method. It reduces fear and the sense of risk and encourages the learner to plunge into the language and swim.

Teachers must respond to all of these types of learning styles for different ages of students, which requires endless creativity and an awareness of how learning takes place in and out of the classroom. Pretending to be on a train in Spain would be great for some fifth graders, whereas an actual ride on a city subway for older students shows how Spanish is used along with English to give directions and emergency instructions. A visit to a French, Italian, Japanese, or German restaurant will provide opportunities for high school students to use their new language skills, whereas making some simplified dishes in home economics would be perfect for middle school students. Newspapers, TV programs, sporting events, and a host of other daily activities can reinforce and stimulate learning for the interested teacher and student.

Working Conditions

The various teaching career paths share much in terms of content knowledge and methodology. However, working conditions do vary dramatically among the teaching options we have cited. A basic difference between schools on the elementary and secondary levels and colleges and professional language schools is the voluntary attendance of students at college and elective curriculums.

Public Schools

Public schoolteachers through the high school level have participated in formal education and teacher training courses to obtain their certification. They have trained in teaching methods and classroom management and have prepared themselves to plan course outlines, select textbooks, assign work over the semester or quarter, and use visual aids and equipment effectively. Public schoolteachers frequently discuss the merits of various teaching methods in their attempt to fulfill the school's curriculum mandate and at the same time inspire and instill knowledge in a group of students who often see school or individual classes as an imposition on their lives.

In public school teaching, attendance and, to some degree, courses are imposed on the students with a resulting constrained effect on interest, motivation, and performance. Public schoolteachers must be skilled classroom managers and sometimes even disciplinarians to accomplish their academic goals. Individual students can be disruptive and seriously compromise entire classroom environments. School incidents of violence can affect all classes, and many schools impose a number of behavior rules that the teacher is expected to enforce.

Public schoolteachers have a more rigid workday, with prescribed arrival and departure times. In some school systems, textbooks and other materials are chosen by the school district or the department chair, and the teacher is expected to adopt those texts and teach from them. In other situations, the individual instructor may choose the textbook. Many teachers are asked to take on extracurricular assignments, such as coaching sports or leading clubs. Much work is taken home in the evening: grading papers, entering marks into the record, writing reports, and planning for future classes. Offices, if they are available, tend to be shared, and space is limited. Support services are limited; teachers often prepare their own exams, copy them, and do much of the administrative work themselves. In less well-endowed public school districts, teachers report buying supplies with their own funds. Meeting with parents, counseling them about their children, and being responsive to them is another distinctive requirement of this level of foreign language teaching.

Private Schools

The role of the teacher in a private school setting is determined by many variables: whether the school is residential or commuter, the cost of tuition, the type of student clientele it attracts, the degree to which the school is tuition-driven or supported by endowments, and any affiliations the school might have. In general, private school salaries tend to be lower than in public schools, although salary is often supplemented with housing and board, which may include the teacher's spouse and children. On the other hand, resident teachers often live in apartments in dormitories or houses on campus and are expected to make evening checks and be available on a more irregular schedule than are public schoolteachers.

In the case of resident campuses, the faculty is part of the school family and is expected to attend all meals (in fact, places may be assigned at certain tables), performances, sporting events, and so forth, to ensure group cohesion and esprit de corps. If your self-assessment indicated you must have significant amounts of privacy in your life or a sharp demarcation between work and home, private school resident positions would be most unattractive to you and could engender serious stress if accepted.

One great advantage of many private schools is the smaller teacher-to-student ratio and the attention and concentration on individual student development allowed by that smaller ratio. There is more time to explore issues and topics and more time to work with students who need extra help. In fact, most private schools have excellent learning support systems that capitalize on their smaller size and familiarity with every member of the student body.

In addition to teaching duties, most teachers are expected to coach a sport or sponsor a significant activity such as theater, school newspaper, literary magazine, outing clubs, and the like. Not all of this is out-of-class time, as private school academic schedules tend to be less rigid than their public counterparts. There may be short days or school holidays devoted to certain events or activities.

Private schools tend to have a number of special traditions, buildings, and features that may be attractive to potential faculty. There is a respect for tradition and the past. Although now less true than before, these schools still tend to maintain rather firm criteria for behavior, dress, and interpersonal conduct.

Colleges and Universities

College-level teachers are hired for their advanced degrees and their scholarship; many have taken no courses in teaching methodology. Most would have experienced some teaching assignments during their graduate programs, either as teaching assistants or by doing part-time adjunct faculty work or teaching contract courses, but some may not have had this opportunity. Their ability to structure a class and fulfill a curriculum is based in large part on the belief that this will be accomplished just as they mastered much of their own advanced study in their subject: through autonomous learning. Nevertheless, many college faculty arrive with less actual classroom experience than high school teachers (who have had required student teaching) and often no experience with technology, visual aids, and textbook purchasing, much less a formal study of teaching methodologies and modalities.

For the college educator at either the undergraduate or graduate level, there is a different audience. Although some undergraduates are required to study a language, they have several languages to choose from. After those minimum requirements are met, most of the student population in upper-level foreign language classes are interested in and dedicated to the pursuit of excellence in that discipline. Classroom management is not an issue, although there is the same need for lesson plans and organization of learning.

College instructors have great freedom in choosing texts, course materials, and class concepts, although they must fulfill the stated intent of the course as published in the college catalog. When several instructors are teaching the same numbered course, they may agree in advance to use the same textbook. This helps to ensure that they meet the same outcome criteria and are fair to students who must change class meeting times. It also helps ensure that students who need this course as a prerequisite for later course work have been presented with similar material and approaches.

The change from high school to college means fewer classes for students overall and particularly fewer classes per day. Because of the college student's smaller class load, students have more time to devote to a subject and can thus improve more rapidly. The college student studying a foreign language, then, has more time during the week to spend working in the language lab and reviewing course materials. College teachers can and do expect more from students and can demand a higher quality of work.

For the student, there may be foreign language film series, student clubs, newsletters, or coffeehouses in which to practice language skills. At one university, the Spanish department holds a weekly Spanish tea, where refreshments are served and only Spanish is spoken in a delightful, easygoing, conversational setting.

There are numerous benefits to working in a college or university setting. Facilities tend to be excellent, and there is usually adequate support staff to type materials and examinations, do copying, and prepare testing materials. A private office is often provided, and there may be a variety of faculty privileges. Computers are provided for writing, research, library access, and data manipulation.

At the college level, teaching is the principal job responsibility, although there is certainly a requirement to serve on committees, both departmental and all-college, for any number of issues, programs, and initiatives. Some hours of faculty advising are generally required to make the faculty member available to students for counseling. With seniority, class schedules and routines in general tend to be to the faculty member's taste. Colleges and universities have strict guidelines for promotion and tenure that may put pressure on the faculty member to write, conduct research, deliver papers at professional meetings, and become involved in outreach to the community and/or college service in order to rise in academic rank or even retain the position at that institution. In some departments, the role of department chair is rotated and all faculty are expected to serve a term. In other institutions, the chair is a contested office.

Professional Language Schools

For the teacher associated with a professional language school, this is essentially a salaried position, full- or part-time depending on the teaching load. Full-time positions tend to involve more classes per day than either public or college teaching, and pay may be based on the number of classes taught. There are not the same associated duties, although lesson planning may still be the teacher's responsibility. In some of these schools, materials, books, and even day-to-day schedules are predetermined as part of an overall system that the school subscribes to.

Because these schools are commercial, support materials tend to be good to excellent. Because students are not in degree programs and pay only for the individual courses, there are no grades. There may be, in fact, a tendency to be relatively uncritical to avoid consumer complaints. Employment may be highly responsive to enrollments, and firm contractual agreements are rare.

Training and Qualifications

As mentioned previously, teaching and certification requirements vary depending on the level at which you choose to teach. This section discusses the particulars for each type of position within the various settings.

Elementary and High Schools

For the elementary school language teacher, the minimum educational requirements would be a bachelor of education degree with certification appropriate to the state. Because certification requirements are constantly changing, contact the ERIC Clearinghouse on Languages and Linguistics (cal.org/ericcll) for a comprehensive discussion of state certification requirements. The Academic Employment Network website (academploy.com) provides a convenient mechanism for checking certification requirements for most states. Be sure to verify the certification information you find on any website, as it may not be up-to-date. In addition, the Modern Language Association (mla.org) recommends that individuals spend time in the country of interest, develop an awareness of foreign language pedagogy, have a supervised teaching experience, have course work beyond the generic education classes, and that their skills in the use of the foreign language be formally assessed.

Colleges and Universities

Most four-year colleges require that job candidates possess a doctorate in the foreign language being taught and might, in addition, look for specialized areas of research, publication, prior teaching, or foreign travel in countries where that language is spoken. Occasionally, a college will hire faculty on a nontenured basis with less than a doctorate degree, but the larger the institution, the less likely that this will be the case.

At the senior levels of graduate work for both master's and doctorate degrees, you will be teaching and working with seasoned scholars who are developing their own unique areas of expertise as they pursue the degree you hold. Classes may be very small at this level, even at a large university, and the work is highly collaborative. Your teaching work at this level may be reduced to allow for pure research and writing in your areas of interest and scholarship. You will be called upon frequently to speak to professional and scholarly groups about that research.

If you are hired without an earned doctorate, there may be a stipulation in the contract at hiring indicating how much time can elapse before the degree must be earned. The difficulty here would be to finish the degree while holding down a full-time job. (For many people, the dissertation is the most challenging and time-consuming aspect of the degree.) This certainly should be considered in your negotiations.

Professional Language Schools

Professional language schools will vary dramatically in what types of qualifications they demand of teacher applicants. In many cases, formal education and training in teaching a foreign language is not necessary. Experience, however, is often preferred. In these institutions, native speakers of a language will find many great opportunities, as learning a language from a native speaker is often part of many organizations' marketing campaigns. Some language institutions even offer study abroad or language immersion programs, which may give you the opportunity to work outside the United States.

Earnings

Public elementary and secondary schoolteachers of foreign languages are paid according to the same salary schedules as other teachers in their school district. Salaries across the nation vary depending on location and are affected by the cost of living and level of state and community support for education as reflected in the school budget. Because published reports on teacher salaries are generally three to five years out of date, contact the National Education Association (nea.org) or your state's Department of Education to get the latest figures available. Public school salaries are public information, so a call to the school district you are interested in will give you the median salaries for each level of degree and for different amounts of experience. In general, according to the U.S. Bureau of Labor Statistics (bls.gov), average teachers' salaries range from $41,400 to $45,920; the lowest 10 percent earn $26,730 to $31,180; the top 10 percent earn $66,240 to $71,370. According to the American Federation of Teachers (aft.org), beginning teachers with a bachelor's degree earn an average of $31,704 during the school year.

Private school salaries are generally lower than those of public school—teachers. On average, public schoolteachers earn between 25 to 119 percent more than private schoolteachers earn. On the other hand, private schoolteachers may receive additional perks, such as free room and board or paid tuition for their children. Additionally, some of the same location factors that affect public schoolteachers' salaries also affect those working in private schools. Unfortunately, there is no good data available to give you a better idea of how much you can expect to make working in a private school.

According to the Bureau of Labor Statistics, earnings for college faculty vary according to rank and type of institution, geographic area, and field. According to a recent survey by the American Association of University Professors (aaup.org), salaries for full-time faculty average $68,505. By rank, the average was $91,548 for professors, $65,113 for associate professors, $54,571 for assistant professors, $39,899 for instructors, and $45,647 for lecturers. Faculty in four-year institutions earn higher salaries, on average, than do those in two-year schools. Earnings also vary depending on the type of institution for which you work, with salaries averaging from $79,342 in private independent institutions, to $66,851 in public institutions, and $61,103 in religiously affiliated private colleges and universities. Many college professors enjoy some unique benefits, including access to campus facilities, tuition waivers for dependents, housing and travel allowances, and paid sabbatical leaves.

There is limited information available for those interested in working for a professional language school. In general, however, these positions receive lower pay than others discussed in this section because there tend to be fewer educational or training requirements for staff. Teachers at these institutions tend to be paid by the hour, instead of a salary, and benefits may or may not be part of the package.

Career Outlook

The National Center for Education Statistics (nces.ed.gov) cites a number of interesting trends that affect public schoolteachers of foreign language. In general, at any given time, there tend to be fewer vacant teaching positions for foreign languages, meaning there are more applicants than jobs. So, although your elementary or secondary teaching degree is a valuable credential, you are entering a highly competitive market and you will need to be aggressive in your job search. The well-prepared job seeker will also be able to discuss current trends in curriculum choices for foreign languages at the elementary and secondary levels.

Private school foreign language teaching positions are expected to see only the growth demanded by a slightly increasing student pool. Hiring will increase only modestly over the next decade. Fortunately, the private school system has always emphasized foreign language in their usually classic curriculums, and the private school market remains a viable alternative for employment in the future. The choice of languages has more breadth in the private schools than in the public schools, and that may be a factor for some candidates.

As for higher education and prospective teaching in foreign language, the Modern Language Association (mla.org) reports that foreign language professors at four-year colleges are employed as follows: 63.7 percent in tenure-track assistant professor positions and 25.2 percent in nontenure-track full-time positions. The remaining are in part-time positions, postdoctorate fellowships, and academic administration. One important trend worth researching as you consider employment in academe is the increasing use of part-time faculty. There are many reasons for the shift, but the bottom line for you means that there is a heavy competition for full-time positions in higher education. Given your investment of time and financial resources, there is much to consider. Both the Chronicle of Higher Education website (chronicle.com) and the American Association of University Professors website (aaup.org) will have the latest information on these topics.

Strategy for Finding Jobs in Elementary and Secondary Public Schools

To secure a teaching post in a market for which supply outstrips demand in many localities argues for approaching the job search strategy with an almost military precision. You need to think of working on several fronts at the same time. All of your activity should be geared to securing an interview with school hiring officials. Given solid interview skills as outlined earlier in this book, the more interview opportunities you have, the greater the probability of your being offered a teaching contract.

One possibility is that the job you really want may not be near to where you currently reside. Consider the question of relocation carefully. If openings are not plentiful in the area where you currently live, seek out information on supply and demand elsewhere and think positively about the advantages of a move. Although there is certainly the risk of the unfamiliar in a move, to have a job that utilizes your education is a wonderful accomplishment. With that under your belt, you can go about putting down roots in a new community, making new friends, and learning the advantages of your new home.

Begin with Your Degree-Granting Institution

Make certain that before you leave campus you have a good understanding of and are registered with all the available placement services. They may be located not only in the career office but also in the school of education offices. Many schools have credentials files, which contain copies of your teaching résumé, your letters of recommendation, and other qualifying documents. As you leave school and begin your job search, the credentials office will mail this packet of materials to anyone of your choosing. There is often a modest fee for this service. Its advantages are its convenience, usually quick response time, and its providing a centralized spot for all your records.

Your college will also be in receipt of job postings from local and state schools for teaching positions. Find out where these job postings are displayed and review them frequently. Apply for every reasonable position. In most cases, you don't really learn about the details of a position until you have the opportunity for an interview, and there will be ample time to discuss details of a job offering.

The public schoolteacher candidate is advised to make a regular practice of scanning all newspapers advertising in and around the geographic region being considered. Newspapers need not be purchased. If a newspaper has a website, job listings can be reviewed online. And most libraries subscribe to a selection of newspapers, both local and national. Be sure to check the Sunday listings on a regular basis.

Expand Your Network of Contacts

Send a cover letter and résumé to schools where you would like to work. State departments of education publish directories of all public schools in the state, including the names of superintendents, principals, and other administrators. Names, addresses, and phone numbers are regularly included in these listings. This information is also generally provided on state websites. In addition, many libraries and college career counseling centers will have this same information on file.

Your college career office or teacher placement center will also have listings of annual teacher job fairs around the country. Take note of any in your area and call or write about registration requirements, fees, and other details. Teacher recruitment fairs often include opportunities to meet principals and superintendents and schedule time for brief interviews that may lead to additional meetings at another time.

Strategy for Finding Jobs in Private Schools

Accessing the private school market is a very different process than seeking a public school situation. In general, there is not a significant amount of crossover between the two systems, and teachers within a private school system tend to stay within that educational environment. Private schools list positions and send out job notices but seldom advertise in newspapers to ensure a more select pool of candidates and maintain a lower profile than their public school counterparts. As tuition-driven institutions, they do not have the core franchise market of students that public schools automatically have and therefore must seek students through reputation and advertising. Consequently, their recruitment and hiring efforts are low-key.

Attend Job Fairs

Find out about job fairs and attend as many as you can. Job fairs for private schools, both here in the United States and abroad, are held year-round. Many are administered by recruiting firms. These fairs serve as a major entrée for many job seekers into the private school system. You register your credentials with a private school placement agency, which then provides access to a private school job fair. There you can meet and interact with a number of hiring officials from a regional or national base. Your college career office can put you in touch with some of these private school recruiting firms or give you a schedule of teaching job fairs around the country.

Consider Placement Agencies

There are many reputable teacher placement agencies around the country, and if your job search becomes particularly challenging, you might consider investigating one of these services. However, before you sign a contract, be certain you've taken it home and studied it to understand all the conditions and costs associated with the services being offered. Many of these firms are providing services that duplicate those your college career office or teacher placement center is providing or can arrange to provide for you at another college through reciprocity agreements.

You can find placement agencies on the Web by checking sites like Job-Hunt.Org's Academia/Education section (job-hunt.org). No matter how you locate an agency, check them out with the local Better Business Bureau, talk to your career office about placement agencies to learn what their experience has been, and find out whether the agency itself will allow you to contact previous clients to discuss their experiences with the agency. All of these efforts will help you to reduce the risk associated with fee-based agencies.

Consider Relocating

You will want to know exactly in which states your certification is valid and try to be as mobile as possible in your job search. Studies have shown that new teachers in their first job often do not relocate more than twenty-five miles from home. Sometimes this decision is financially driven when new-teacher salaries make it difficult to rent an apartment, finance and insure a vehicle, and pay all the associated expenses of living away from home. However, every year teaching districts do without teachers because they are too rural or too remote for consideration by some candidates. Ironically, often these job sites will provide not only the warmest welcome for a needed teacher but also the supportive atmosphere and climate so important to a new recruit in a demanding position. What these locales may lack in services, they may make up for in a lower cost of living and an opportunity to make a difference in young people's lives.

Strategy for Finding Jobs in Colleges and Universities

Acquiring a college teaching position nearly always demands that you relocate to an institution other than where you received your degree. Higher education has limited openings at any one time, and part-time work or adjunct faculty status at one institution is no guarantee of earning a full-time spot. Most departments have budget lines dedicated to full-time, potentially tenured faculty. This means that faculty who are hired in those budget lines are expected to become a permanent part of the faculty and earn tenure and promotion when they qualify. Consequently, although there may be schools you would enjoy teaching at or areas of the country you would prefer, the supply and demand for college professorships usually will require you to relocate.

Go to the Source

The Chronicle of Higher Education (chronicle.com) is the weekly national publication listing junior college, four-year college, and university teaching positions in foreign language. Many of these advertisements are large display ads that detail in full the requirements and duties of the positions advertised. Your career center, department office, and college library will have copies you can review each week.

Network with Faculty Colleagues

Another excellent source of college-level positions will be the faculty colleague contacts you make as you pursue your advanced degree. There is a well-established network that becomes active when schools are seeking to fill a position. A personal recommendation from a friend or former teaching associate will be welcomed by faculty at the hiring institution. For this reason, it's important to ensure that your faculty mentors and colleagues are well aware of your teaching and research interests and geographic preferences so they can respond for you and move the process along if an opportunity presents itself.

Attend Professional Meetings

Interviews are often conducted at professional meetings, where recent job openings may be announced or posted in a conspicuous place at the registration table. As a graduate student, many of these conferences are available to you at substantially reduced fees or no fee at all. You should take advantage of them for the professional content and the opportunity to meet representatives of departments at other institutions.

Strategy for Finding Jobs in Professional Language Schools

Professional language schools are located in large metropolitan areas where they can be close to their principal market. Their clients include international travelers and businesspeople, students seeking to enhance regular academic work in a language or to take a refresher course for examinations or travel, and individuals seeking self-improvement. To enlist students, these schools must advertise heavily. Check Sunday editions of metropolitan newspapers, or search the Internet using the Big Book search site (bigbook.com) for the state where you want to work.

Additional Resources

Teaching has become an intensely competitive field, with supply in many disciplines far outstripping demand. There are a number of considerations to keep in mind as you seek an employer. Your principal goal is to teach your language at the educational level you have trained and prepared for. If that is not possible, the next easiest transition would be to accept a different grade or age level. If that is not available, consider using your teaching credentials in a different way. In the public schools, this could mean teaching in another content area (with provisional certification), substituting, or serving as an aide until something permanent appears in the school district. At the college level, it may mean part-time instructing as an adjunct faculty member until an opening occurs.

In teaching, the possible employers are fortunately very well documented. Below, we have identified resources that can provide the names of potential employers.

Directories
Patterson's Elementary Education and *Patterson's American Education* are annual lists of public and private elementary and secondary schools, school districts and superintendents, postsecondary schools, and others, including nursery schools, YMCA programs, and the like. Use these directories to conduct your proactive job search activities: mailing out cover letters and résumés, networking, and telephone follow-up.

Private schools are identified in the *Handbook of Private Schools* (Porter Sargent Publishers). Visit your local library to browse through these resources, as they can be quite expensive. Another good resource is *Independent School*, the journal of the National Association of Independent Schools (nais.org). It is published three times a year and contains articles on issues of concern to private schools as well as a number of display advertisements.

Professional Associations
Be sure to carefully review the websites of the professional associations for teachers of foreign languages listed at the end of this section. Many associations offer job listings or job search advice for members.

Related Occupations

Some related occupations will allow you to directly use your language skills, as teaching does, while others may only allow occasional use of your language expertise. These related occupations include the following:

ESL Teacher   Translator/Interpreter
Import/Export Agent   Hotel Manager
Airline Customer Service Agent   Travel Agent

Teachers share certain personality traits with other types of workers, according to Holland's theory of careers. If you are considering other types of work, be sure to read job descriptions for the following:

Librarian   Undercover Agent
Passenger Service Representative   Claim Agent
Volunteer Services Director   Production Agent

Professional Associations

As you will see in looking through the following list, there is an association for nearly every language that is taught. Draw on these associations to find out about job listings and to enhance your professional skills.

American Association of Teachers of Arabic
wm.edu/aata/index.php

American Association of Teachers of Esperanto
tejo.org/aaie

American Association of Teachers of French
frenchteachers.org

American Association of Teachers of German
aatg.org

American Association of Teachers of Italian
aati-online.org

American Association of Teachers of Spanish and Portuguese
aatsp.org

American Association of Teachers of Turkish
princeton.edu/~turkish/aatt

American Conference for Irish Studies
acisweb.com

American Council of Teachers of Russian
americancouncils.org

American Council on the Teaching of Foreign Languages
actfl.org

Association of Teachers of Japanese
colorado.edu/ealc/atj

College Language Association
clascholars.org

Modern Language Association of America
mla.org

National Association for Bilingual Education
nabe.org

National Council of State Supervisors of Foreign Languages
ncssfl.org

Teachers of English to Speakers of Other Languages (TESOL)
tesol.org

7

Path 2: Translating and Interpreting

In using your foreign language skills in translation or interpretation, you are using the language as a primary skill. Positions using foreign languages as a primary skill require a comprehensive grasp of the language and the cultural context of that language. Gertrude Stein taught us to appreciate beauty and not labels when she wrote, "A rose is a rose is a rose." Knowing your literature is one thing, but could you quickly quote something comparable to this famous line in the foreign language you have studied?

To achieve the necessary fluency to work as an interpreter or translator demands extensive study of the language, perhaps periods of time as a resident of a country using that language, and a complete grasp of the cultural context, literature, music, economics, and history of those who speak that language. A simultaneous interpreter of Spanish, for example, represents the apogee of the art of moving instantaneously between two cultures. A quote from Shakespeare in English might be rendered immediately into something appropriate from Cervantes, and vice versa.

Even with the requisite language skills, your work in translating or interpreting might take you into new and unexplored areas. For example, medicine, science, ecology, and anthropology each would represent a specialized vocabulary to be mastered and concepts to be understood. Constant study and acquisition of these knowledge bases is a hallmark of the superior practitioner of translation or interpretation.

Definition of the Career Path

Interpreters and translators are needed all over the world where peoples of differing cultures and languages come together, either physically, on the printed page, or through some other medium. Publishers, educational institutions, hospitals, trade organizations, and governments all have need of interpreters or translators at some point.

Translators deal with written documents and interpreters with oral expression. Some translators work in only one direction, for example, from Japanese to English, whereas others are comfortable translating in either direction. Interpreters, on the other hand, because they are involved in social situations, are often called on to communicate in both languages. The highly skilled and justifiably famous simultaneous interpreters of the United Nations (un.org) work very intently in relatively short shifts interpreting in one direction. They rotate several interpreters to maintain concentration and because each interpreter must produce an approved text of his or her work for that shift.

Most interpreters translate from one or two passive languages into an active one—their mother tongue. The best definition of "mother tongue" may be the language in which nursery rhymes are familiar. Interpreter positions frequently call for a degree in foreign languages, a minimum fluency in three languages (mother tongue included), and successful scores on written and oral examinations.

The Benefits of Living Abroad

Even entry-level positions for translators or interpreters emphasize superior language skills and will seldom compromise on this aspect of the job specification. There may be both written and oral tests of your language skills by other foreign language practitioners. Many interpreters and translators speak highly of the fluency skills they gained by living abroad in a geographic area where that language is spoken exclusively. You should seriously consider this an important, but not necessarily academic, part of your job preparation.

If you are in high school, speak with your guidance counselor about the Experiment in International Living (usexperiment.org) and similar programs that will place you with a family in another country while you go to school there for a year. Many alumni of this program make lifelong friends and return to their placement site often throughout their lives and host their families and friends on visits to the United States. More important, diligent students find it gives them a quantum leap in language skills and cultural understanding.

Your college may have existing exchange programs of its own or may belong to a consortium of schools that share academic year or semester abroad programs. Tuition is usually similar to your regular school tuition, but room, board, and transportation will almost always represent an increased cost. These programs allow you a chance to continue your education and experience living in a foreign country. Many graduates of these programs recommend investigating the options carefully. Some are disappointed to find their foreign schooling is actually an American experience; Americans are grouped together, the program is essentially comprised of English speakers, or it is difficult to make contact with native speakers and the culture.

Even if your classes are in English, check out off-campus living arrangements in boarding houses, pensiones, or small hotels that may offer attractive long-term rates. This will allow you to inhabit a neighborhood, meet some locals, and experience life away from your academics. The American Institute for Foreign Study (aifs.com) publishes a large catalog of programs each year for Austria, China, France, Germany, Italy, Mexico, Spain, Russia, and a number of English-speaking countries as well.

Short-term working experiences in service occupations can be arranged through the long-established Council on International Educational Exchange (ciee.org). It places students in jobs in France, Germany, Costa Rica, and some English-speaking countries. It provides assistance with job placement, visas, work permits, and inexpensive overseas airline flights.

The Need for Superior English Skills

Love of and proficiency with the foreign language under consideration are not the only criteria for success. The essence of interpreter/translator positions is effective communication, and that means superior skills in your own language and culture. Because no one language can be easily translated into another, interpreters and translators must do the best they can to convey accurately the essence of the language. For this reason, there is usually ongoing debate in translator/interpreter circles about the words and citations from literature that may or may not have been the most effective choice in a particular translation.

Given the breadth of possible choices in effective and meaningful translation or interpretation, it follows that the individual performing this transformation must have at his or her command all the possibilities inherent in the English language as well. Translators and interpreters need mastery of a variety of syntactical structures, comprehensive vocabulary, encyclopedic knowledge of literary and musical allusions, and a solid grasp of the history and sweep of English language and literature as embodied in written and spoken forms. Add to this requirement the daunting fact that often the knowledge of one or more additional languages is necessary for success in the field. In both Eastern and Western Europe, there has been such a tradition of cultural interchange and flow between nations that to limit yourself to one language could restrict your possibilities for employment.

As the economy grows more global and as people everywhere begin to appreciate cultural pluralism, the need for skilled individuals to bring us together and allow us to make meaning of our interactions will continue to grow. Interpreters and translators are bridge builders, connecting cultures, minds, thoughts, beauty, and science between two worlds. It is an exciting, worthwhile career—and a needed one!

Possible Job Titles

Interpreters and translators are usually called just that. There are some specializations within these fields, and other job titles you may see include linguist, language specialist, précis reporter, literary translator, conference interpreter, and judicial interpreter/translator.

When you are interested in using your language skills to interpret or translate as a secondary job function, any number of job titles can apply. A federal visa applications office might hire a secretary who speaks French fluently, an administrative assistant who can translate Spanish, and a director who is fluent in German. These are just three of the hundreds of possible examples of job titles to consider. Use the information contained in this chapter to help you brainstorm a list of possible job titles.

Possible Employers

There is a range of employers who hire workers to use foreign language skills as either a primary or an auxiliary job function. These employers include professional language schools, publishers, hospitals, federal government agencies, state and local governments, foreign firms operating in the United States, American firms operating in foreign countries, U.S. manufacturing firms exporting to or importing from other countries, translation agencies, and other employers.

Professional Language Schools
Professional language schools often offer translating and interpreting services; check the Yellow Pages on the Internet under "Language Schools" to find potential employers in a specific city.

Publishers
Literary translators work for publishers under either an authorial or a work-for-hire agreement. Approximately 1,500 translated books are published each year in the United States; this number has not changed significantly in the past ten years and is not expected to. The top book publishers in the United

States are Random House (http://randomhouse.com), Simon & Schuster, Inc. (simonsays.com), Penguin Putnam, Inc. (penguinputnam.com), Time Warner (twbookmark.com), HarperCollins (harpercollins.com), Wiley & Sons (http://wiley.com), Houghton Mifflin (hmco.com), and W.W. Norton (wwnorton.com). Moody's directories (see "Additional Resources" section in the back of this book), other corporate directories, and the Yellow Pages for metropolitan areas can be used to identify additional publishers that you may be interested in contacting.

Hospitals
Nearly every hospital that serves a sizeable population of non-English speakers has interpreters on its staff. Hospitals consider interpreters to be a critical component in generating new income for the facility by providing a valuable service to non-English-speaking patients and their families, thus making the hospital more marketable to the public. Some large hospitals employ ten to fifteen interpreters, depending on the number of languages used in the community and the number of people using those languages. Again, the Yellow Pages are an excellent resource for identifying hospitals in a given geographic region.

Federal Government
The federal government, even with budget cutbacks and extended hiring freezes, is still a very large employer. Future budget cutbacks will affect the number of entry-level government positions available, but there continues to be a need for federal employees. Various federal government agencies hire individuals with in-depth knowledge of cultures, geographic regions, and languages. These agencies include the Defense Intelligence Agency (dia.mil), Voice of America (voa.gov), Drug Enforcement Administration (dea.gov), National Endowment for the Humanities (neh.gov), Library of Congress (loc.gov), National Security Agency (nsa.gov), and Federal Bureau of Investigation (fbi.gov).

State and Local Government
Interpreters, translators, and others with language fluencies work in many capacities for state and local governments. Just a few of the possibilities are described here. Contact your state's personnel office and talk with an employment specialist about other possibilities. You can locate all state personnel offices through the website at statelocalgov.net.

States fund social service agencies that serve new immigrants and non-English-speaking people. These agencies hire interpreters and more specifically trained workers, such as social workers, who are fluent in at least two languages. Check with the appropriate state personnel office for more information on the types of positions available and regions of the state where those workers are employed.

Some economic development offices, or arms of those agencies (international trade centers or offices), interact with officials representing both U.S. and foreign firms. There is often a need for translators and interpreters to assist in importing and exporting goods and services, and many of these state offices compile lists of individuals and firms who provide translation services. Contact your state economic development office for more information on how you can be included on its list. State courts also need to make use of the services of freelance translators and interpreters in the courtroom.

Foreign Firms Operating in the United States

The *Directory of Foreign Firms Operating in the U.S.,* published by Uniworld Business Publications, lists companies by home country, alphabetically by company name, and alphabetically by American affiliate. This volume is an invaluable resource for identifying organizations in which foreign language skills could play an important role in your employment. Check your local or school library for a copy.

American Firms Operating in Foreign Countries

A three-volume directory titled *Directory of American Firms Operating in Foreign Countries,* also published by Uniworld, lists companies alphabetically by company name and by the foreign country in which they do business. As with the *Directory of Foreign Firms Operating in the U.S.,* this is an excellent resource for identifying companies that present opportunities for using a foreign language, either as a primary or an auxiliary job requirement and you should look for it in your nearest library.

Translation Agencies

Translation agencies like Berlitz Translation Services (berlitz.com; located in every major city) and others hire workers on a freelance basis. These companies can work with up to two hundred freelancers a year. Ninety percent of these people translate from some other language into English. Translation agencies usually hire experienced workers, and when they need to bring on additional translators, they ask for names from the people they are currently working with. Most of these agencies can be found in New York; Washington, D.C.; Chicago; Dallas; and San Francisco. Use the Yellow Pages and Web Yellow Pages to locate organizations in your area; they may be listed under "Translation Agencies" or "Translators and Interpreters."

Other Employers

Many other types of employers hire translators and interpreters. They include airlines, law firms specializing in patents or immigration, shipping companies, travel agencies, banks, TV networks, radio stations, museums, advertising agencies, and foundations such as the Red Cross or the Ford Foundation. Consult with library professionals you are working with to find appropriate resources that will allow you to develop a list of companies or agencies to contact.

Working Conditions

Many literary translators are self-employed, or, like their counterparts who do interpreting on a freelance basis, they have another occupation to support them, perhaps a teaching position or work in publishing or editing. Some U.S. corporations employ both translators and interpreters on a full-time basis, but the total number employed full-time in the commercial sector remains only in the hundreds. The U.S. government, through its agencies, also employs significant numbers of interpreters and translators. Many government employees are former military personnel who gained their language training or additional significant language skills at the Defense Language Institute Foreign Language Center (dliflc.edu) in Monterey, California.

The consequences of not finding full-time work as an interpreter or translator are twofold: first, you must be prepared (and qualified!) to be employed in some other capacity. This suggests other skills and talents that you can market to an employer that are perhaps not connected in any way with foreign languages and interpretation or translation. Second, you must have working conditions that will allow you to continue to do the necessary marketing to seek self-employment for your foreign language skills. This might mean making phone calls, sending out letters or brochures, or even being able to leave work briefly for an interview or meeting. Juggling a full-time job and staying available for translating or interpreting projects can be difficult. The alternative of not using your foreign language skills, even in a part-time manner, and risking loss of fluency may be equally disagreeable and unacceptable.

Working exclusively as an interpreter or translator in a less than full-time capacity means having a strong tolerance for low job security. Benefits will be nonexistent, except perhaps during periods of extended employment, and there may be weeks or even months during which you are unemployed. Additionally, it is difficult to be actively seeking freelance positions if you are working at another freelance position full-time. The cycle may become work, no work, seeking work, working again.

There are important differences in working conditions between interpreters and translators. Interpreters, by the nature of their work, must work at the venues where their services are required (e.g., the conference table, in a hospital setting, at an international media fair, or within university colloquium). Their work is immediate; very involved with personalities, nuance, and subtlety. They work on their feet, at meals, and on the move. They work exposed to all around them and often under intense pressure.

Translators, on the other hand, can work in libraries, at home, or in quiet offices, crafting their work alone and wrestling with problems and discovering solutions in private. Freelance translators also work on-site at conferences and symposia to prepare written materials, including edited transcripts of speakers, panels, and discussions.

Both types of jobs can involve significant amounts of travel and demand flexibility and the willingness to handle the problems associated with travel. Interpreters especially, and to some degree translators as well, must be prepared to set up housekeeping and work stations anywhere.

Interpreters and translators often specialize in a particular area (e.g., science, medicine, literature), but it is obvious that the more broad their interests, vocabularies (in their nonnative tongue), and experiences, the more work opportunities may present themselves. Although you may be working regularly as a translator of medical texts, if you are willing to broaden your horizons, you may find substantial additional translation work in other fields. For example, recently there has been heightened interest in ethnic knitting traditions, and more American knitters are seeking Andean, Norwegian, and Chinese knitting patterns. Children's literature from all over the world has become popular, and the demand for skilled translators in this field has increased. Opportunities present themselves to those who seek them.

Training and Qualifications

We have emphasized throughout this discussion of translating and interpreting careers that a superior level of skill in your native tongue, in addition to fluency with the written and oral expression of the foreign language, is essential. In the case of simultaneous interpretation, speed and accuracy are critical. Consecutive interpretation, in which the translation occurs following the speaker, places emphasis on the interpreter's memory.

Whatever the role, both positions argue for excellent academic preparation in language, grammar, punctuation, and syntax. Foreign language training should begin as early as possible. A college degree is essential for these types of positions. Take as many foreign language courses as possible, but don't neglect writing and speaking courses in your own language. If you are interested in working in a particular subject area (e.g., politics, economics, literature), then take additional courses in that area as well.

In addition to your traditional academic preparation in high school and college and possibly graduate school, there are a number of specialized schools and institutes where you can acquire specific and intensive language skills suitable for interpreting and translating positions. There are many professional language schools that can provide training, but the Modern Language Association (mla.org) recommends that you undertake a program of study offered by an institution of higher education. A professional language school's program will gladly teach you how to ask for a ham sandwich in Arabic, but they may not tell why that is inappropriate. However, if you believe a professional language school will meet your needs, check the Yellow Pages under "Language Schools" for programs available in your area.

The following colleges and universities provide training at the certificate to master's degree levels in interpretation or translation:

American University, Washington, D.C.—Certificate in translation
Bellevue Community—College—Certificate in translation and
    interpretation
College of Charleston—Master's degree in bilingual legal interpreting
Columbia University—Master's degree in Russian translation
Florida International University—Certificate in legal translation and
    court interpreting
George Mason University—Certificate in translation
Kent State University—Master's degree in translation
Monterey Institute of International Studies—Master's degree in
    translation/localization management and translation and interpretation
New York University—Certificate in court interpreting
    (Spanish/English) and translation
Rose-Hulman Institute of Technology—Certificate in technical
    translation
Rutgers University, New Jersey—Master's degree in Spanish, option in
    translation
San Diego State University—Certificate in Spanish/English translation
Union County College in Elizabeth, New Jersey—Certificate in
    interpreting spoken language
University of Arkansas—Master's degree in translation
University of Binghamton, New York—Master's degree in comparative
    literature for literary translation
University of Florida—Certificate in translation

University of Iowa—Master's degree in translation
University of Massachusetts, Amherst—Master's degree in translation
University of Milwaukee—Master's degree in translation
University of Minnesota—Certificate in interpreting with health-care
    specialization; certificate in interpreting with legal specialization
Wake Forest University—Certificate in Spanish translation/localization
    and interpreting

Earnings

Earnings for translators and interpreters vary widely. For those employed full-time by U.S. government agencies, pay at the entry level is in the mid-twenty thousand dollar range; senior-level positions with the government can pay as much as $60,000. Corporate jobs have a slightly higher starting salary and can, with seniority and promotional raises, provide salaries comparable to and higher than government jobs. Corporate positions, however, even long-term ones, may be only for the duration of a particular project.

Most translating positions are freelance with no benefits. Rates are billed by the word, the hour, or the job. Hourly rates can fall between $15 and $30, and a highly skilled translator can earn between $60,000 and $150,000 per year. Conference interpreters often work for a flat fee for that conference, up to $500 a day.

Online translation services charge from one to four cents per word. Some translation specialists associate with a firm that will do advertising, billing, and serve as a central booking office. While contract translators working under these situations may make less than freelancers, they do not have the overhead for advertising and promotion that independent agents do.

Career Outlook

In the United States, job opportunities for full-time translators are limited. Some of the variables that affect demand are the skill level of the translator/interpreter and the languages of fluency. There is more demand and less supply for Khmer than for French, for example. The largest employer of translators is the Foreign Broadcast Information Service, part of the Central Intelligence Agency (cia.gov). Most of the translators work at home, sending and receiving work electronically.

Europe may provide a better market for translators but not necessarily American translators. U.S.-educated students compete with citizens of European countries with excellent training in English as well as fluency in their native tongues and often several other languages. Additionally, most European Community (EC) members must first hire from their native labor pool before hiring foreigners (U.S. citizens). Asian countries also have well-established English language programs beginning in elementary school, and fluency in English increases each year with these populations.

There are many large placement agencies in Europe that operate similarly to temporary employment agencies in the United States. Students may work temporarily without a work visa, but placement agencies in Europe report that students seldom are perceived as contractors for translators or interpreters and usually do not fill these types of positions. Nonstudents must have a work visa to work at all, and to gain such a visa, guaranteed employment with a foreign employer is required.

No matter who the employer is, most of the demand for interpreters and translators is less than full-time. As a result, individuals hired to perform these functions usually need other skills and attributes to recommend them to a hiring organization. The translating or interpreting role is certainly important but only intermittent.

Strategy for Finding the Jobs

Creativity is the watchword for finding jobs in translating and interpreting. We have discussed the educational background and language fluency requisite for interpreters and translators. Let's assume the ability to move effortlessly between languages is one of your skills. How do you get started on a career in translating or interpreting? Where are the jobs, who will hire you without experience, and how, then, do you get that experience?

Whether you are seeking permanent staff employment in a civilian or government situation or are willing to risk the exigencies of a freelance career, you'll need to begin acquiring experience as soon as possible, even while you're in school. Call and write your local hospitals, schools, and Chambers of Commerce. Let them know you are available to translate or interpret for visitors or guests who have difficulty with English. In some communities, orchestras, choral groups, and even schoolchildren visiting foreign countries on educational or cultural programs might appreciate the voluntary services of an interpreter or translator. Some of these organizations may be able and willing to cover your transportation expenses. As you acquire some of these experiences, ask for letters of reference to begin to build a portfolio and résumé to support a more substantial job search.

Being reactive and watching for job advertisements in newspapers is another resource you certainly should use. After all, you know there is a job opening when you see an ad, you know what qualifications and experience are being requested, and you're told exactly how to apply. Log on to about.com and under the "Jobs & Careers" section you can locate jobs listed by individual states or you can check out the classified sections of newspapers around the country.

In addition to Web surfing the classifieds, don't forget to check out some of the bigger websites devoted to jobs for recent college graduates, such as careerbuilder.com and monster.com.

Networking is another key strategy for finding jobs in interpreting and translating. Let people know you are seeking work and ask to be recommended by those you have worked with on past projects. When attending conferences, meet and talk with as many of your colleagues as possible. Be sure to have some simple business cards made up with your name, language proficiency, address, and telephone number to pass out as a reminder. The International Labor Organization (ilo.org), a large user of interpreters, has a staff of resident interpreters to draw from, yet it uses freelance interpreters 80 percent of the time. Often, one freelancer is asked to recommend others to the employer.

Joining professional groups such as the American Translators Association (atanet.org) opens up additional opportunities, including that of becoming credentialed. These organizations not only provide the opportunity to network with colleagues at national, international, and regional meetings, but also publish newsletters and annuals that contain important editorial material and display ads from employers, programs, schools, and organizations offering products. Student membership is modest.

Being well organized and detail oriented will help you in your job search. Keep excellent records of your contacts, get back in touch with people promptly, and treat everyone as a potential client. Consult with clients thoroughly to understand their needs, format specifications, and all associated details before tackling a job, and then meet all deadlines. Have distinctive stationery and billing forms made up. Even your answering machine message is an indication of your professionalism and seriousness of purpose. Clients easily generalize from these outward image associations to conjectures of the quality of your work.

Finally, reading books, practicing your skills using tapes and videos, and attending films, conferences, and training sessions all improve your fluency and general information level. Take advantage of any and all opportunities to get better at what you do. Your jobs may range from conferences on polymer chemistry to apiary techniques. You cannot afford to be ignorant of vocabularies or concepts.

Related Occupations

The skills required to be successful in translating and interpreting are also needed in other kinds of jobs, including news editing, news directing, reporting, technical writing, newscasting, and creative writing. According to the *Dictionary of Holland Occupational Codes,* the personality traits associated with people working as translators are similar to those of people working as microbiologists and bursars. Interpreters are like lawyers, brewers, producers, artist's managers, and recreation supervisors (to name just a few) in terms of personality traits. In looking at related occupations or occupations that draw on your strengths, abilities, and values, use what you discovered about yourself in the self-assessment portion of this book to consider all the possibilities.

Professional Associations

There are myriad professional associations that individuals interested in interpreting or translating can join. Membership in these organizations can provide many benefits: a better understanding of what working in the profession is really like and current challenges facing the profession, notification of opportunities for additional training and professional development, inclusion in a directory that potential employers might use for hiring purposes, and access to actual job listings or referrals. If you would like to find out more about any of the following organizations, check out their websites.

The American Association of Language Specialists
taals.net

American Literary Translators Association
literarytranslators.org

American Translators Association
atanet.org

Buddhist Text Translation Society
bttsonline.org

International Association of Conference Interpreters
aiic.net

International Association of Conference Translators
aitc.ch

International Federation of Translators
fit-ift.org

Israel Translators Association
ita.org.il

Modern Language Association of America
mla.org

National Association of Judicial Interpreters and Translators
najit.org

Northwest Translators and Interpreters Society
notisnet.org

Society of Federal Linguists
federal-linguists.org

8

Path 3: Government

There are a variety of options for foreign language majors seeking employment with local, state, or the federal government or one of many governmental agencies. This chapter explores options in each area and discusses how to navigate the complex application and interview process to land one of these stable and highly coveted jobs. Take time to explore the U.S. government websites, both those included in this chapter and links you discover during the course of your own research; you may find more career options than you thought possible.

The Federal Government

It does not take much exploration of how to use a degree in foreign languages to recognize the employment possibilities in the U.S. government. The federal government, even with frequently discussed reductions in force, employed more than 1.9 million civilians (excluding those at the U.S. Post Office) in 2004. Almost all (96 percent) were working in the executive branch, which includes the Executive Office of the President; fifteen executive cabinet departments, including the Department of Homeland Security; and nearly ninety independent agencies, each of which has clearly defined duties. Government workers can be found in tens of thousands of agencies, boards, bureaus, commissions, and departments across all three branches of government—the executive, legislative, and judicial. The kinds of people hired reflect the nature of the work done in a particular unit. Government agencies hiring the largest numbers of college graduates range from Veterans Affairs to Education, from Treasury to Energy. Federal jobs are much more likely to be white-collar, professional, or administrative positions than is true in the economy overall.

Another consideration in seeking government employment is the nature of government agency work and the desired qualifications of candidates for that work. Specialized education and training, which includes training in foreign languages, is required for many of these positions. Initially, it can be a challenge to determine specific qualifications that the government is seeking. It will take some follow-up on your part to find out which jobs require the skills you possess.

Many government agencies and departments need foreign language expertise, if not as a primary skill, then as an important auxiliary talent. This chapter will look at a number of both of these possibilities with the caveat that agency needs change frequently, especially in today's global village. A government agency that previously had little need for employees with foreign language skills may now have a requirement for them.

The government screening process takes skill, care, and lots of questioning to complete satisfactorily. This may help to weed out those who are easily discouraged, who have difficulty doing research, and who find forms and documents an impossible challenge. The government employment process does play a part in self-selecting good candidates because it can be quite tricky to maneuver through. A sample of recent job listings showed the following requirements:

- Each applicant must submit a separate completed application for federal employment (SF-171), optional application for federal employment (OF-612), or a résumé for each grade or compensation level you wish consideration for, listing your work duties and accomplishments relating to the job for which you are applying.
- Candidates are to submit (1) an application (e.g., SF-171, OF-612, résumé, etc.) which is signed and dated; (2) an OF-306, Declaration for Federal Employment (if submitting OF-612 or résumé); (3) a DD-214 if claiming a five-point veterans" preference, an SF-15 if claiming a ten-point veterans' preference, Certificate of Release, or other claims; (4) transcripts, memberships, and other affiliations; and (5) an SF-50 (if applying as a transfer or reinstatement eligible).
- You will be required to complete a Declaration for Federal Employment (OF-306) to determine your suitability for federal employment and to authorize a background investigation. You will also be required to sign and certify the accuracy of all the information in your application.
- If selected, male applicants born after 12/31/59 must confirm their selective service registration status.

- A background security investigation will be required for all new hires.
- You must successfully complete a thorough medical examination, a polygraph interview, and an extensive background investigation.

If language skills are a job requirement, you will see a statement in the job listing similar to the one shown below:

Applicants for this position must be bilingual in English and Spanish. Candidates must be able to communicate in English and Spanish with individuals for the purpose of obtaining information and conveying an understanding of complex requirements of federal programs. The ability of potential candidates to communicate in English and Spanish will be determined in an interview conducted in English and Spanish. Candidates who do not have the ability to communicate in English and Spanish sufficient for successful performance in the job will not be eligible for the position.

Don't let these kinds of requirements put you off! The federal government and civil service jobs in general can provide solid employment prospects. Government jobs can provide excellent income, superior working conditions, and, to many who are employed in this sector, an ambience no different from any major employer. If government employment is not on your list to explore, consider adding it.

Federal Departments and Agencies

The federal government continues to hire new college graduates to fill full-time, permanent positions as well as temporary and part-time positions. Every government agency fills these positions, and an increasing number of them require fluency in a foreign language. Some of the larger federal agencies and departments that hire workers with language skills are described below.

State Department. The State Department (state.gov), founded in 1789, is the lead federal institution for the conduct of American diplomacy. The department hires foreign-service officers, foreign-service specialists, and civil-service employees. Applicants interested in a foreign service career will take a written exam and an oral exam, which is made up of three parts: a group exercise, a structured interview, and a case management writing exercise. Fluency in certain foreign languages may qualify candidates for language incentive pay while serving at posts where these languages are spoken. The department's website provides the details you'll want to know as you explore this option.

Central Intelligence Agency. The CIA (cia.gov) services the United States as an invaluable source of information on trends and current events abroad. It is the agency that coordinates our nation's intelligence activities by collecting, disseminating, and evaluating foreign intelligence that affects our national security. Most CIA positions are located in the Washington, D.C., area and salaries are administratively determined. Because of the sensitive nature of this department, applicants undergo a rigorous process of screening, including medical, psychiatric, and background investigations and a polygraph interview. Interested applicants should visit the CIA's website to learn more about working for the CIA and to review current job openings.

Bureau of International Information Programs. The Bureau of International Information Programs (IIP) (usinfo.state.gov) is the principal international strategic communication service for the foreign affairs community. The office is part of the State Department. IIP designs, develops, and implements a variety of information initiatives and strategic communication programs, including Internet and print publications, traveling and electronically transmitted speaker programs, and information resource services. These reach— and are created strictly for—key international audiences, such as the media, government officials, opinion leaders, and the general public in more than 140 countries around the world. Visit the website to learn more about the office and then visit the State Department's website to learn more about current jobs and hiring procedures.

Voice of America. For more than fifty years, the Voice of America (VOA) (voa.gov) has provided news, features, and music to its international audience. Competing with nearly 125 similar broadcast services worldwide, VOA is one of the top international broadcasters in today's vast global media market. Each week eighty-six million listeners around the world tune in to VOA programs that are broadcast in fifty-two languages, including English, via direct medium wave (AM) and shortwave broadcasts. Millions more listen to VOA programs placed on local AM and FM stations around the world, giving VOA a vast and unequaled global reach. VOA also offers TV programming and information via the Internet. For current employment information, visit the VOA's website and review advertisements for international radio and TV broadcasting positions.

Citizenship and Immigration Services. Under the Department of Justice, the U.S. Citizenship and Immigration Services (uscis.gov) is both a law-enforcement and service-oriented agency with a wide range of responsibilities over the admittance, processing, and possible exclusion of aliens with respect to citizenship in the United States. Some of the major occupations in the agency are border patrol agent, inspections officer, investigations agent, detention and deportation officer, information technology specialist, and a number of administrative jobs. Many positions require the ability to speak or learn Spanish and other languages. Visit the website for more information, then follow the instructions given to view current job postings.

Department of Defense. The Department of Defense (DOD) (defenselink.mil) provides the military forces needed to deter war and protect the United States. The major departments of this unit are the Army, Navy, Air Force, Marine Corps, Coast Guard, National Guard and Reserve, and the Department of Homeland Security. With hundreds of thousands of civilian employees, there is a broad range of employment possibilities and the need for a variety of preparations, including a foreign languages background. Visit the Department's website to learn more about hiring options.

Peace Corps. Founded in 1961 by President John F. Kennedy, the Peace Corps (peacecorps.gov) is an international development agency of the federal government. It places volunteers in countries throughout the developing world in a variety of projects. Currently, more than 7,800 Peace Corps volunteers are serving in seventy-five countries, working to bring clean water to communities, teach children, help start small businesses, and stop the spread of AIDS, to name just a few projects. Since its founding, more than 182,000 Americans have joined the Peace Corps, serving in 138 nations. The appreciation of another culture through foreign language training is valued by the Peace Corps. Its website shows current openings and guides you through applying online.

National Endowment for the Humanities. In 1963, Congress enacted the National Endowment for the Humanities Act (neh.gov) to promote progress and scholarship in the humanities and arts in the United States. This grant-making agency supports research, education, and public programs in the humanities. In order to accomplish its goals, the agency hires some workers with either a bachelor of arts or master of arts degree in languages or linguistics for program specialist positions. Visit the Office of Personnel Management's website (opm.gov), select NEH as the agency, then view current job listings.

Department of Justice. The Department of Justice (usdoj.gov), which includes the Federal Bureau of Investigation and the Drug Enforcement Administration, hires individuals with language fluencies. This department employs thousands of people throughout the world who are responsible for carrying out law enforcement functions and providing legal services to the government. To review a listing of departments and vacancies, visit the Department of Justice's website.

Definition of the Career Path

Entry-level career opportunities in the federal government are widely advertised, and detailed job specifications are available for all but the most classified occupations. Although the application process may initially appear to be challenging, the screening and interview processes are fair and impartial, and diversity is encouraged. Entry-level positions are classified according to government pay grades, and promotions and advancement opportunities are clearly indicated. Unlike many civilian occupations, the career path in most government jobs can be well defined. During your interview process you should be prepared to discuss the career path possibilities with representatives of the agency or department to which you are applying.

As mentioned previously, advancement for most workers in the federal government is currently based on a system of occupational pay levels, or "grades," although more departments and agencies are being granted waivers to experiment with different pay and promotion strategies. Workers typically enter the federal civil service at the starting grade for an occupation and begin a "career ladder" of promotions until they reach the full-performance grade for that occupation. This system provides for a limited number of noncompetitive promotions, which usually are awarded at regular intervals, assuming job performance is satisfactory. The exact pay grades associated with a job's career track depend upon the occupation.

Typically, workers without a high school diploma who are hired as clerks start at grade 1, and high school graduates with no additional training hired for the same job start at grade 2 or 3. Entrants with some technical training or experience who are hired as technicians may start at grade 4. Those with a bachelor's degree generally are hired in professional occupations, such as an economist, with a career ladder that starts at grade 5 or 7, depending on academic achievement. Entrants with a master's degree or Ph.D. may start at grade 9. Individuals with professional degrees may be hired at the grade 11 or 12 level. Those with a combination of education and substantive experience may be hired at higher grades than those with education alone.

Once nonsupervisory federal workers reach the full-performance level of the career track, they usually receive periodic step increases within their grades if they are performing their jobs satisfactorily. They must compete for subsequent promotions, and advancement becomes more difficult. At this point, promotions occur as vacancies arise, and they are based solely on merit and in competition with other qualified candidates. In addition to within-grade longevity increases, federal workers are awarded bonuses for excellent job performance.

Workers who advance to managerial or supervisory positions may receive within-grade longevity increases, bonuses, and promotions to higher grades. The top managers in the federal civil service belong to the Senior Executive Service (SES), the highest positions that federal workers can reach without being specifically nominated by the president and confirmed by the U.S. Senate. Relatively few workers attain SES positions, and competition is intense. Bonus provisions for SES positions are even more performance-based than are those for lower-level positions. Because it is the headquarters for most federal agencies, the Washington, D.C., metropolitan area offers the best opportunities to advance to upper-level managerial and supervisory jobs.

Working Conditions

It is difficult and not particularly responsible to generalize about federal government employment. Certainly, we have indicated in this section that the application process, even learning about job openings, is an indication of the size and complexity of the employer. But once hired, can it be so different from any other job? Yes and no. The federal government shares many of the advantages and disadvantages of a very large employer. There is bureaucracy, red tape, some enforced mobility, and some loss of personalization. There are also excellent salaries, benefits, career advancement possibilities, training programs, and mobility opportunities. The advantages are largely in the regularity and stability of government employment.

Many federal employees will tell you that the working conditions are no different from the private sector. In fact, most government jobs have more regular hours and make less after-work demands on their staff than does the private sector. Working hours are fairly standardized. The working environment, however, may not be as luxurious as the private counterpart. Spending in government positions is complex and purchases come through numerous channels, so working environments tend to be fairly standard to spartan in decor and quality.

Training and Qualifications

If you take time to visit the Office of Personnel Management's website (opm.gov) and look through the entry-level professional or managerial job listings, you'll find that many specify the qualifying education as "any four-year degree." For example, when investigating civil-service jobs in the U.S. State Department, the website says that any B.A. or B.S. degree is useful for their job opportunities. The job announcement shown below does not specify an exact set of credentials but rather shows the kind of background required of applicants.

> *International Radio Broadcaster, D.C. Knowledge of Kurdish people and American foreign policy required; for more information and application materials contact: Bureau of Broadcasting, Personnel, Washington, D.C.*

Office and administrative support workers in the government usually need only a high school diploma, although any further training or experience, such as a junior college degree or a couple of years of relevant work experience, is an asset.

Once employed, each federal department or agency determines its own training requirements and offers workers opportunities to improve job skills or become qualified to advance to other jobs. These may include technical or skills training, tuition assistance or reimbursement, fellowship programs, and executive leadership and management training programs, seminars, and workshops. This training may be offered on the job, by another agency, or at local colleges and universities.

Earnings

Federal employees are paid according to one of two major pay systems: the statutory pay systems or the other major pay systems. There are three statutory pay systems that include the General Schedule, Foreign Service, or Veterans Health Administration systems. Other major pay systems include the Federal Wage System, the Executive Schedule, an Administratively Determined system, and the Senior Executive Service pay system. The three systems most pertinent to this discussion are the General Schedule, Foreign Service, and Administratively Determined systems. What this means is your pay is largely preset based on the nature of the job you're hired to do. Your job and your experience in a job are assigned a level and your pay will correspond accordingly to that level. You can find a complete discussion of these systems in various reports available on the Office of Personnel Management's website (opm.gov) under the "Employment & Benefits" or "HR Tools & Resources" tabs.

Those paid according to the General Schedule (GS) are largely white-collar, professional, administrative, scientific, and technical employees. Entry-level positions for most college graduates begin at the GS-5 or GS-7 level. A schedule has been established for within-grade advancement, and once you become a government employee, your eligibility for positions at a higher grade is enhanced. Foreign Service pay plans and schedules have been established for officers (pay plan FO) and personnel (FP). Within this pay system, the lower the class number, the higher the pay. Foreign Service positions are typically even more competitive than General Schedule positions and may require rigorous background checks that often take a year to complete. Entry-level salaries are correspondingly higher.

Salaries are competitive with the private sector except for some specialized positions that may not do as well in the federal pay scales as they would in the private sector. Otherwise, regular pay raises, advancement, and promotion are largely apolitical, and benefits and pension plans are competitive.

Many college graduates are disappointed when they review the entry-level salaries that are paid to many of the federal employees. The value of the benefits received, the relative stability of employment, and the defined system that provides for advancement when performance merits it, are attractive enough to keep federal employment very competitive. The following table will begin to give you a sense of the amount you can earn when working for the U.S. government. For definitions of the GS level, refer to the previous section in this chapter, "Definition of the Career Path." Although the most current GS pay scale can be found on the Internet, at the time of this printing the following pay information was available:

FEDERAL GOVERNMENT GENERAL SCHEDULE PAY RATES, 2005

GS Level	Entrance Level	Step Increase	Maximum Level
1	$16,016	Varies	$20,036
2	18,007	Varies	22,660
3	19,647	$655	25,542
4	22,056	735	28,671
5	24,677	823	32,084
6	27,507	917	35,760
7	30,567	1,019	39,738
8	33,852	1,128	44,004
9	37,390	1,246	48,604
10	41,175	1,373	53,532
11	45,239	1,508	58,811
12	54,221	1,807	70,484
13	64,478	2,149	83,819
14	76,193	2,540	99,053
15	89,625	2,988	116,517

Source: U.S. Bureau of Labor Statistics, U.S. Office of Personnel Management.

Drawbacks to Government Employment

Critics could easily take some of the advantages of federal employment and portray them as disadvantages. For example, the stability and regularity of government salaries are seen by some as a distinct disadvantage. If the economy does well or an individual excels dramatically in his or her job, the private sector can reward performance with increases in salary. That is not possible in a federal job. Let's look at some other frequent complaints.

Bureaucracy. So much paperwork, so many rules, and so many individuals who have made careers from mastering these complex forms and procedures can be frustrating to those who want to cut through red tape and get a job done. Many would say that the bureaucracy discourages risk taking, innovation, and creativity.

Politics. The government is responsive to the political party in office, without a doubt. This response, however, is rather diffuse and slow. New administrations can bring about large-scale changes in government management, but many day-to-day decisions are compromised by political considerations. Critics charge it's not what's best that is considered, but whose political interest holds sway.

Public Esteem. Federal employees and the jobs they do are not generally held in high regard in the United States. Because their efforts do not have the visibility of the private sector, which uses mass media to single out star performers and successful organizations, they are not perceived as interesting or as active in their field. The relationship of the federal budget (including federal salaries) to income taxes is always a subject of public debate, and some people see federal employees as an additional burden on the tax rate.

Career Outlook

Federal hiring may not be as immediately reactive to economic conditions as is private industry, but federal hiring does follow shifting national concerns and priorities. Given the priorities of the administration in power, some departments and agencies will grow while others will shrink. Even so, this is a competitive employer whose labor force by all standards is better educated, is more technically astute, and has higher language and math skills than the workforce as a whole. Positions are competitive, and, in spite of the number of positions available to any four-year graduate, there is definitely a bias toward individuals with scientific, computer, and other quantitative skills.

In general, government statistics project that employment in the federal government will grow by 2.5 percent through the year 2014, compared to 14 percent growth projected for salaried employment in all industries combined. The reason job growth will be slower in the federal government than in the private sector is because increased homeland security needs may be largely offset by declines in other federal sectors due to governmental cost cutting, the growing use of private contractors, and continuing devolution—the practice of turning over the development, implementation, and management of some programs of the federal government to state and local governments.

Foreign language majors considering government positions that do not rely on language skills could maximize their attractiveness as job candidates by acquiring some additional technical skills while in college. If your quantitative ability has been something you've enjoyed using in the past, take advantage of some related mathematics courses, for example, statistics, linear programming, and perhaps some research design courses, if available. A few of these would make an impressive addition to your degree. But perhaps mathematics has not been a strong point. Try computers. Take more than the basic introduction course. Talk to a computer science advisor about what two or three courses would work well together for you as a nonmajor.

Keep in mind that these are only two possible options. While there will be job openings in all types of jobs over the coming decade, demand will continue to grow for specialized workers in areas related to border and transportation security, emergency preparedness, public health, and information analysis, so you might want to tailor your education accordingly. In addition, the distribution of federal employment is expected to continue to shift toward a higher proportion of professional, protective service, and business and financial operations workers. Employment declines are projected to be the greatest among office and administrative support occupations as well as production occupations, due to increasing office automation and contracting out of these jobs.

Finally, keep in mind that government jobs are less likely to be immediately responsive to fluctuations in the economy. While there have been some eliminations of government departments over time, the general picture is one of security. Individual jobs, too, must be highly compromised to warrant an employee's replacement. The appeal and grievance procedures are detailed, and abrupt individual job loss is rare, except for malfeasance or gross misconduct.

State and Local Governments

State and local governments also need foreign language talent. State and local governments employ about 7.9 million workers, placing them among the largest employers in the economy. Seven out of ten of these employees work for local governments, such as counties, cities, special districts, and towns.

A large city with a shipping port and foreign docking potential may desire someone with foreign language experience to help develop trade and to market its docking and stevedore services. A state economic development office seeking industry to locate within its boundaries might develop a task force for the promotion of industrial sites to foreign manufacturers. The individual who brings a knowledge of a foreign language to these kinds of teams provides an invaluable service.

The need for workers with foreign language skills has become much more pronounced at all levels of civil-service employment, including states, cities, towns, and municipalities. Police officers in even midsize cities may find growing communities of people speaking Spanish, Thai, Laotian, or Chinese. Doctors, nurses, social workers, and many officials find knowledge of another language to be a plus in their work and in their job enjoyment.

State Government

Many state jobs mimic the federal level to a remarkable degree. Depending on the size of the state and the bureaucracy established, the system may be as complex and multitiered as the federal government. However, unlike the federal government, there is apt to be a central personnel office (usually in the capital city) and branch personnel offices that list all state openings and can provide specifications sheets for each of these positions. These "spec sheets" list required qualifications or combinations of experience and education necessary to apply, salary schedules, and whether or not a test is part of the application process. Examine the following job ad, which shows various combinations of education and experience that are acceptable for those interested in applying.

Workers' Compensation Claims Supervisor. The [state] Department of Labor has a permanent, full-time position. Successful candidate will perform responsible administrative, supervisory, and technical duties as they relate to workers' compensation law. Minimum qualifications: Bachelor's degree in related field. Also two to three years' experience in business management, insurance operations, or related field. Experience in processing insurance claims, supervising, or any equivalent combination of education and experience.

Visit a state personnel office, in person or via the Internet, and learn how to file a formal application, read the current job postings, and then stay abreast of additional postings. In some states you can file one application and indicate the kinds of jobs you want to be considered for, and your application will become part of those applicant pools for a period of time.

If you know where you want to work in state government, visit that location, meet the people associated with the office, and express your interest. Bring a résumé or arrange for a formal interview. However, a word of caution is due here. This is best done ahead of any formal job posting. To make such a visit after a job is announced would be disadvantageous for you and deemed inappropriate by personnel in the state office.

The state personnel office can be of great assistance in explaining the various state agencies and directing you to more information about the mission of each of them. Remember, their job is to secure the best-qualified applicants for the state, so they're interested in raising your level of awareness and appreciation of state government.

Local Government

Nowhere will your curiosity, perseverance, and research skills serve you better than in your search for a job in local government. Unlike the federal and state systems, local governments conform to no overall system; each is different, and informal aspects of a job search (talking directly to local officials) may be far more important here than the formal application process.

There are county governments, towns, cities, villages, unincorporated villages, boroughs, locations (New Hampshire), and plantations (Maine). There are school districts and special districts for water, fire services, sewage, and a number of other missions. The composition, names of offices, and structures of these various governing organizations are idiosyncratic. The various structures have evolved over time, and the only similarities tend to be in the areas of local government involvement. Education, health care, highway maintenance, police, fire, parks and recreation, and sewage and water quality are among the frequently encountered areas of local government concern.

There is no one strategy for approaching this diversity of local government organizations. Some small towns' hiring practices are very informal, and a résumé and request for a formal interview might actually work against you. Other government organizations have job postings, application processes, and pay-scale systems that rival their federal and state counterparts. You must assess each local government structure individually and decide on your best approach. Once again, sharing with people what you are looking for, asking lots of questions, and using local reference sources (such as the local library and its staff) will educate you on the kinds of jobs available, what it might take to fill them, and what kind of application process is used.

Working Conditions, Training, and Qualifications

Working conditions, training, and education for jobs working with a state or local government are no different than for those with the federal government.

Please review the pertinent sections within the "Federal Government" section above for more details.

Earnings

Earnings vary by occupation, size of the state or locality, and region of the country. As in most industries, professionals and managers earn more than other workers. It's almost impossible to state how much you can expect to earn in a position within a state or local government since the positions themselves are so varied. Similar to working for the federal government, benefits and job security tend to be fairly high, which often compensates for a lower pay scale.

The following is a table that shows the average salaries for a few of the professionals working in local governments. Keep in mind that, while your foreign language skills may come in handy in some of these positions, a foreign language degree alone will not be sufficient to land you the job.

MEDIAN ANNUAL SALARY FOR SELECTED EXECUTIVE AND MANAGERIAL OCCUPATIONS IN LOCAL GOVERNMENT, 2004

Occupation	Salary
City manager	$88,695
Assistant chief administrative officer	80,232
Information services director	75,582
Engineer	75,556
Chief financial officer	74,867
Economic development director	70,668
Public works director	70,135
Fire chief	70,000
Human resources director	70,000
Chief law enforcement official	69,837
Human services director	64,832
Parks and recreation director	62,988
Health officer	61,536
Purchasing director	59,013
Chief librarian	56,270
Treasurer	52,053
Clerk	46,779

Source: Bureau of Labor Statistics

The table on this page describes the median earnings for the occupations with the most workers within state and local governments. These earnings are listed as hourly wages.

Career Outlook

According to the Bureau of Labor Statistics, employment in state and local government is projected to increase 11 percent through 2014, slower than the 14 percent growth projected for all sectors of the economy combined, but faster than that at the federal government level. Job growth will mainly stem from the rising demand for services at the state and local levels. An increasing population and state and local government assumption of responsibility for some services previously provided by the federal government are fueling the growth of these services. Despite the increased demand for the services of state and local governments, employment growth will be slightly dampened by budgetary constraints due to the rapidly increasing proportion of revenues devoted to the Medicaid program; reductions in federal aid, especially at the county level; and public resistance to tax increases. Outsourcing of government jobs to the private sector will also limit employment in this sector. When economic times are good, however, many state and local governments increase spending on programs and employment.

Professional and service occupations account for over half of all jobs in state and local government. Most new jobs will stem from steady demand for community and social services, health services, and protective services.

MEDIAN HOURLY EARNINGS OF THE LARGEST OCCUPATIONS IN STATE AND LOCAL GOVERNMENT, EXCEPT EDUCATION AND HEALTH, 2004

Occupation	State Government	Local Government
Police and sheriff's patrol officers	$23.55	$21.64
First-line supervisors/managers	19.68	20.24
Family and school social workers	16.86	19.53
Correctional officers and jailers	16.22	15.90
Firefighters	14.94	18.78
Highway maintenance workers	14.81	14.10
Maintenance and repair workers	13.80	15.70

Source: Bureau of Labor Statistics

For example, increased demand for services for the elderly, the mentally impaired, and children will result in steady growth in the numbers of social workers, registered nurses, and recreation workers. There will also be strong demand for information technology workers. Foreign language students can be particularly helpful in these areas.

Possible Job Titles

The range of possible government job titles would constitute a volume on its own, so we offer just a few examples. Using information provided throughout this book, add titles while you do your own customized research.

Federal
Foreign Service Officer
Foreign Service Specialist
Passport Examiner
Career Trainee
Junior Officer Trainee
Writer/Editor
International Visitor Exchange Specialist
Academic Exchange Specialist
News Assistant
International Radio Broadcaster
Border Patrol Agent
Immigration Inspector
Special Agent
Personnel Manager
Program Specialist

State
Administrative Assistant
Program Coordinator
Assistant Director
Assistant Manager
Program Monitor
Analyst
Program Aide
Program Assistant
Inspector
Investigator
Supervisor

City/County/Local
Administrative Analyst
Administrative Assistant
Program Analyst
Planner
Investigator
Inspector
Office Manager
Counselor
Program Planner

Strategy for Finding the Jobs

The end result—obtaining one of the many excellent government jobs for individuals with foreign language degrees—more than justifies the means. Admittedly, the process includes a challenging and sometimes frustratingly detailed and complex set of applications and job posting and hiring rules. It can become a job in itself just to master the various systems. Try to remember that the government—federal, state, or local—is made up of people just like you. They are interested in your application. So, if the going gets tough, and it probably will, ask for help.

Personalize Your Search

Successful government job seekers have indicated that one way to break through the bureaucracy is to personalize your efforts. Begin by calling the agencies or departments you are seeking employment with and speak to a representative of each. Tell him or her what you're doing and ask for assistance and guidance. This will put a voice and a name to the employer, and he or she will certainly have valuable advice about the job specifications and other details of the job that interest you. Of course, you'll want to be careful not to ask for any special consideration or treatment for your candidacy, simply information on the position and the application procedure.

Uncover All the Job Listings

The government job market is unlike any other. Consequently, your job search strategies here will be different as well. Your first task will be to ascertain that you are seeing as many of the available job postings as you can, because no one location, website, listing, or hotline carries complete coverage of government, especially federal, job openings. If you are a persistent job seeker, plan to check each of the relevant sources described here. Become familiar with each and determine how often new jobs are listed so that you can create a postings review schedule for yourself.

Federal Jobs

A good place to start looking for actual job listings is on the U.S. Government's Office of Personnel Management website (opm.gov). This site explains the federal employment process, and lets you look at current job openings, get general information on federal agencies, and submit an online application.

Several federal agencies were highlighted earlier in the chapter, and their specific website addresses were listed. Remember, not all federal vacancies are listed on the OPM's site. So if you don't see any job listings for a specific agency where you would like to work, be sure to locate its website and review job vacancies listed there.

Follow Up as You Would with Any Other Employer

Following up on your federal, state, or local government application is just as important as it is in the private sector. You can verify that your materials were received, show the hiring official that you are committed to your job search, and remind him or her that you are qualified and available for employment. If you haven't yet visited the office or agency you would like to work for, and you are able to do so, now is the time to put a face with one of the many applications that these offices receive. Show them who you are and tell them how you can help accomplish their mission given your training, skills, and abilities.

A common impression is that applicants for jobs in the government sector undergo a more formalized screening process. Because of the highly structured classification of employees in these sectors, most applicants believe that once you submit your application, there is little you can do but wait out the process. Yet government employers are no different from any others. When faced with a hiring decision, they want to employ the best person for the job and one that will make a nice fit with the existing organization. Although potential employee application processes and hiring conditions are certainly more codified than in the private sector, that does not mean you cannot put a face to your application or a voice to your name with a visit or a phone call. If you are near enough to visit a potential employment site, by all means do so. Introduce yourself and indicate that you are seeking employment or that you have an application under consideration. You may get a tour and an opportunity to meet some staff. Be sensitive to any concerns others may have that the hiring process is being disturbed. If so, simply withdraw graciously. Finally, if a telephone call is all that is feasible, maybe someone will speak with you about the mission of the particular office you are applying to and talk about current projects and initiatives, if that is possible. Your interest will be appreciated.

Professional Associations

No matter which occupation you may choose to enter, at least one association will be in existence to serve your professional needs. Some of these associations will be able to assist you now by providing possible leads for networking or actual job listings. Look for groups that have membership directories or some type of job listing service. For the most part, you will have to join an association to take full advantage of related services, but if you know that is the field you want to enter, consider it an investment in your future. If you're not sure what type of government work you will seek, review the following list of government-related associations to get an idea of what's out there:

American Federation of State, County, and Municipal Employees
afscme.org

American Foreign Service Association
afsa.org

Civil Service Employees Association
csealocal1000.org

Federal Managers Association
fedmanagers.org

Government Finance Officers Association of United States and Canada
gfoa.org

International City Management Association
icma.org

National Association of Government Communicators
nagc.com

National Association of Government Employees
nage.org

National Association of Governmental Labor Officials
naglo.org

National League of Cities
nlc.org

Society of Government Meeting Planners
sgmp.org

9

Path 4: Educational Administration

One of the most delightful and exciting aspects of studying a foreign language is meeting and communicating with people from different cultures and regions of the world. In fact, that very well may have been your reason for selecting foreign language as a course of study in college. Maybe the language itself was the enticement. You enjoy getting inside another cultural context and being able to communicate. Or, you may find the study of another language a new and exciting way to connect with people. Your foreign language instructors in high school and college may have been born and raised in another country, or they may have spent extended periods in residence abroad, and you probably found that exciting and stimulating. Maybe you met foreign exchange students from other countries who spoke the language you studied. Or you may have had an opportunity to visit another country and practice your language skills on the spot. No matter what your range of experience, you were drawn to learn more about other peoples and how to communicate with them on their terms.

These connections can be created or facilitated in many ways. Teaching may not be what you want to do, or perhaps your educational progress in the language is not sufficient qualification for a teaching career. Traveling and living outside the United States may or may not be an option for you. Nevertheless, you love your language studies and the understanding it has brought you. You want to stay involved with the language, the culture, and, most of all, the people who share your interests. If this sounds like it might apply to you, then the field of educational administration is a career path worth exploring.

Definition of the Career Path

To those wondering just what kinds of careers there may be in administering educational programs, how many programs there are, and what level of diversity exists, take a stroll through your local library or go exploring on the Internet; it will prove instructive. A number of magazines and journals are devoted to education exchange programs, both for study and employment. More and more Americans are discovering internships, foreign travel through established programs and groups, and study abroad programs for summers, vacations, and school terms. All have a pronounced positive impact on education and career development. Each of these programs requires administrators who care about the introduction of American youth into another culture or foreign youth into American culture and strive to make it a positive experience for participants on both sides of the exchange.

The following is a list of educational administration environments, each of which differ in work settings, salary levels, nature of the work, and advancement tracks:

- American-sponsored private schools abroad
- Foreign study exchange programs
- American college programs abroad
- International student programs
- Corporate programs for foreign transfers
- International not-for-profit organizations

These environments all share a belief in the value of experiencing other cultures. However, the programs in the list above are cited because foreign language training is not the principal hiring qualification. Each environment will make different demands on the foreign language graduate in terms of needed and desired qualifications. The job advertisements shown below will begin to give you a good sense of the various demands.

> **Assistant Director of International House and Programs, State University.** Duties: Assists in directing the International House programs and services to international students; provides leadership for the program members; secures qualified students, both American and international, and supervises their activities; solicits and manages funds for the programs and coordinates activities with the International House Foundation and its supporters; assists all

International House students on J-1 visas and provides assistance to the general international student population on F-1 visas. Provides cultural orientation for international students; provides academic advisement and orientation to the university community; speaks and corresponds with outside exchange agencies, university faculty, organizations that support the International House, members of professional organizations, and others; reads and assists with the implementations of U.S. State Department and others. Reads and assists with the U.S. State Department and other appropriate INS regulations, student scholarship applications and forms, and NAFSA documents. Drafts reports including annual report of goals and activities, annual budget, five-year plans, and required federal reports. Qualifications: Bachelor's degree in related field, with master's preferred. Must meet qualifications set by U.S. Department for issuing student visas. Must possess a valid driver's license. International living experience and practical foreign language fluency are preferred qualifications.

Project Assistant, Europe and Eurasia Division, Washington, D.C.
A U.S.-based nonprofit development organization that advances the pace of progress in emerging democracies and developing countries seeks candidates. Duties include providing administrative support to projects, maintaining files and responding to information requests, acting as liaison between Washington and field offices, and supporting proposal development activities. Bachelor's degree required. Russian or European language and computer skills preferred. Good verbal and written skills are a must.

Placement Services Coordinator, Au Pair in America. Responsible for matching host families in the United States with au pairs coming from thirty-eight different countries. Position requirements: Customer service and sales experience required. Ability to work effectively on the telephone and handle multiple priorities is vital. Excellent verbal, listening, and problem-solving skills are important. Must have good data-entry and writing skills. Experience with Microsoft Word, database systems, e-mail, and Internet helpful. Minimum bachelor's degree required.

State University, Coordinator of International Admissions; $3,290 to $3,960 per month. Office of Admissions is seeking a qualified individual to coordinate, develop, and implement standards and guidelines; review of international and domestic transcripts, financial statements, and related immigration documents according to CSU, university, and federal guidelines; counsel and advise prospective and admitted students regarding nonroutine, borderline, and complex situations. Qualifications: Graduation from a four-year college or university in a related field. At least one year of progressively responsible professional student services work experience. Requires application, résumé, and supplemental questionnaire. Call to request application package for Job #00 SA 030.

American-Sponsored Private Schools Abroad

An extensive network of private elementary and secondary American-sponsored schools abroad duplicates almost every aspect of traditional American schools. Each school needs skilled and sensitive administrators to work in non-U.S. settings. Whether it be the Middle East, Europe, or the South Pacific, these schools need administrators, coaches, teachers, and guidance counselors to ensure the American-sponsored school provides an enhanced cultural awareness. Because of the homogeneity of the student and staff backgrounds, it would be all too easy for these communities to become replicas of traditional American culture and values with little interchange or exchange with the communities in which they are located. Administrators with a love of foreign language and culture will provide the leadership needed to bring these schools in contact with the communities they share.

Cultural exchanges are frequently made when American schools celebrate holidays and invite local schoolchildren or residents to participate by viewing a Christmas pageant, a reenactment of the first Thanksgiving, or a mock presidential election. But it can also be accomplished by sharing school facilities with local residents when needed for civic events such as fairs or dances, or by opening up concerts or lectures to the public. Each of these bridge-building activities further entrenches the school in the community as a recognized and valued resource and not a foreign appendage.

Foreign Study Exchange Programs

The college division of the American Institute for Foreign Study (aifs.org) is a good example of a national organization that provides comprehensive information on hundreds of college foreign study exchange programs. Umbrella organizations such as this need staff members who understand the important transition that study abroad programs represent for an American student. Many exchange program staff members bring their own foreign study experiences into constant use on the job and share techniques with prospective students and parents for increasing the likelihood of foreign study being a rewarding and successful experience.

Because many foreign study exchange administrators have participated in these educational experiences themselves, they understand and appreciate the many practical issues of living abroad that need to be resolved before students can get on with the experience of learning. They may suggest places to live where participants can experience a real neighborhood setting or family atmosphere that will allow the student an opportunity to improve speaking skills and idiomatic vocabulary. These administrators can also direct students to vacation or weekend trips to destinations of cultural, historical, or artistic interest that might have been overlooked. They will provide advice on transportation, clothing, living expenses, and many other topics that they have tried and perfected.

If you are interested in autonomy, self-direction, and and being proactive in your work environment, you will find it in foreign study exchange program administration. Jobs such as these may not rely on or even require fluency in a foreign language, but that doesn't mean language skills are unimportant. You will use your language skills on the telephone, in interactions with people, and in writing letters, but not as the single most important aspect of what you do.

Working as a foreign study program administrator in the United States will allow you to use your foreign language degree and experiences to help new generations of students successfully enjoy studying overseas. American staff with foreign language backgrounds work with academic program staff abroad to ensure, on the part of the host institution, successful transitions to a new environment. The gifted individual who has the foreign language training of the host country, an appreciation for and knowledge of the culture, and yet a shared cultural past with the American students becomes the best of guides into a new and exciting world.

American College Programs Abroad

It has become almost a standard expectation of many high school seniors that the colleges they are considering will have some program for exchange study or resident study abroad in one or more countries. Many U.S. universities have established branches in one or sometimes many countries. Even smaller schools can participate with other similar institutions in consortium programs that share curriculums and overseas facilities.

Administrators for these programs need to be more than paperwork experts. They need to know all about the destinations of the students they are advising. They may be asked to advise on the language skill level needed for success, the level of culture shock that might be encountered, or the challenges for the student in a new country. In addition, these administrators are an authoritative voice for the students interested in this experience.

International Student Programs

Here in the United States, all large and many midsize colleges and universities have staff specializing in international student's concerns. Staff members are drawn from candidates who have an interest in international students, are pursuing a career in student affairs, and who have had foreign travel or residential experience, either academic, personal, or through a program such as the Peace Corps. Staff members in these positions help foreign students integrate into campus life by providing counseling, tutorial assistance, directories of on- and off-campus services, placement assistance for part-time employment or spousal employment, and social activities. An important part of their job is creating events to express and share the cultural plurality their students bring to the campus community. They often coordinate groups of local residents who will serve as hosts and friends of foreign students while they attend the American institution.

Corporate Programs for Foreign Transfers

Just as student affairs professionals help to integrate foreign students into the life of the university and surrounding community, corporate liaison specialists do similar work for Americans working abroad.

Many international corporations maintain large staffs in foreign cities including Paris, Brussels, Tokyo, Beijing, and Moscow. Families who follow a working member to these cities rely on foreign liaison staff to teach them the ins and outs of a new culture. It includes familiarizing family members with transportation issues, introducing children to schools, assisting in procuring housing, and providing information about recreational activities and shopping. While liaison personnel may be considered invaluable for locating a source of American peanut butter, they also know what's good on a sushi bar, a satay stand, or a pirogi tray.

These positions are often called "education officer," and the individuals filling these roles will produce informative "fact sheets" and informational brochures and papers on all aspects of the host country's culture. They will produce workshops and provide background materials for corporate planning efforts. Their efforts determine, in large measure, how happy and comfortable employees are in their new surroundings and how the corporate presence adapts to life in a new country. In addition to their liaison duties, these individuals may have other assignments within the human resources area.

International Not-for-Profit Organizations

Not-for-profit organizations that operate abroad also provide job opportunities well suited to foreign language majors who do not want to use language skills as their primary capability but still want to work with another culture. Home offices in the United States and site offices abroad service many volunteer workers. For example, WorldTeach (worldteach.org), a nonprofit nongovernmental organization based at Harvard University, provides volunteer opportunities to those who are interested in teaching in developing countries. This organization recently advertised for home-office staffers who are interested in using their foreign language proficiency. The nonprofit sector is an exciting and growing field of employment that gives its workers lots of opportunities and challenges and the risks and rewards that come with extending oneself and striving for great things with limited resources. In this area of employment, individuals are encouraged to stretch and grow as they help to fulfill the mission and goals of the organization that employs them.

There are nonprofits organized around religious beliefs, political ideologies, human values, and educational aims in science, medicine, language, birth control, disease prevention, agriculture, and natural resources preservation. Bikes Not Bombs (bikesnotbombs.org) recycles bicycles to promote nonpolluting and equitable transportation. The Boston Mobilization (bostonmobilization.org) organizes grassroots support for peace and justice issues. The Network in Solidarity with the People of Guatemala (http://nisgua.org) is a group of local committees supporting grassroots initiatives for economic and social justice in Guatemala. The International Medical Corps (imcworldwide.org) is a nonsectarian, nonpolitical medical organization that provides medical assistance and health-care training in developing countries.

Although all of these organizations do important work, because pay scales on the average tend to be below their commercial counterparts and resources and supplies are less abundant, it is critically important that employees care deeply about the work they do as individuals and believe in the overall mission and goals of the organization.

Possible Job Titles

As you examine the following list of possible job titles, you'll see that many of them are director or coordinator positions. Be sure to also consider assistant or associate director positions or assistant coordinator jobs that you see advertised.

Coordinator of International Students
Junior Year Abroad Coordinator
Program Assistant
Director of Summer Programs Abroad
Program Representative
Director of Administration
Assistant Dean, International Services

Director, International Students and Scholars Office
Director, International Office
Director, Division of International Programs Abroad
International Education Director
Director of Study Abroad Programs
Director of Programs Abroad
Program Coordinator
Director, Academic Programs
Foreign Student Advisor
Visiting Student Counselor

Possible Employers

These career paths are essentially made up of similar jobs in administration that are educational in setting or purpose and are situated either within the United States or abroad. Your search for possible employers can be highly creative. Because the possible employers in the educational administration paths range from private study abroad consortia to traditional public and private schools and colleges as well as the nonprofit sector, you will be locating employers through a variety of sources. You'll find many American four-year college and university positions listed in *The Chronicle of Higher Education*. Not-for-profit positions might be found listed in the Sunday want ads of a major metropolitan newspaper or in a specialized job listing. Corporate liaison positions will be trickier to locate. These positions will be advertised as human resources positions, and the foreign liaison work may be in addition to other duties and responsibilities. Call consulates and embassies and read periodicals in which possible employers might advertise. And don't fail to use the career center at your alma mater or to investigate the possibility that some alumni from your college might be doing the very job you are looking for. They'll want to help you and often can provide valuable advice. Finding the types of employers discussed in this chapter will require you to become an employer detective. Here are some clues to start your search.

American-Sponsored Private Schools Abroad
A word about employment agencies: We have noted before that most of what an employment agency does can be done just as easily and far more inexpensively by a determined and creative individual. That is not the case, however, in the area of private school administration abroad. This employment sector is most often entered through the medium of a teacher/administrator placement agency that gains entrance for its clients to job fairs. There are many reputable firms in the marketplace, they are not difficult to find, and, for the

administrator seeking work in a private school abroad, they may be necessary. Many advertise in the newspapers and journals that service this educational setting, such as *Independent School* or *The International Educator* (tieonline.com). The most reputable are willing to provide client references whom you can contact to hear firsthand about their placement experiences.

Entering the private school administrator market will challenge your perseverance, but once gainfully employed in the private overseas school network, you will notice a continual, and even expected, rotation of teachers and administrators among the various countries. Reading some of the publications that document these moves, such as *TIE* and *International School Services,* you will notice careers that have ranged all over the globe.

Foreign Study Exchange Programs

Saint Michael's College (smcvt.edu) has created a great website that was designed for students interested in studying abroad, but there is also a lot of useful information for you, the job seeker.

There are three organizations to contact if you are interested in working in foreign study exchange program administration. Contact information for these agencies follows:

- American Institute for Foreign Study (College Division) (aifs.com)
- People to People International Headquarters (ptpi.org)
- College Consortium for International Studies (ccisabroad.org)

American College Programs Abroad

In addition to the following representative list of possible employers, the job seeker for positions representing American colleges abroad will find it difficult to assemble a comprehensive list of schools having foreign programs. Some are full-year programs, some are just for a term, and others are only for the summer. There are schools and colleges that maintain complete branch campuses and others that house their programs under the auspices of a resident college in another country. There are also consortia of American colleges supplying students to the same program.

- Brethren Colleges Abroad (bcanet.org)
- Monterey Institute of International Studies (miis.edu)
- Schiller International University (schiller.edu)
- School for International Training (sit.edu)

International Student Programs

Most of these positions will be listed with a variety of titles in *The Chronicle of Higher Education* (chronicle.com). The job seeker will find even small colleges responding to whatever cultural diversity may present itself in their student enrollment. The growth for this particular field promises to be excellent, and more schools feel a responsibility to support cultural pluralism on their campuses and to ease the transition of students from other countries.

Corporate Programs for Foreign Transfers

Individuals seeking employment as liaisons for corporate relocation abroad should keep several points in mind. First, although your ultimate aim is to work abroad, you may have to begin by learning your job and the organizational norms here in this country. Many corporations reserve foreign postings for individuals who have paid their dues by working in the United States. More important, staffs are leaner abroad, and given the distance from the home office and the importance placed on them as representatives of their country, individuals posted abroad need to have earned the company's trust through an established service record. Second, corporate liaison positions are seldom hired off the street through a general job advertisement unless a firm is hiring a foreign national in the area of operation. These positions tend to be hired from existing staff either in the United States or abroad who have displayed a particular interest and knowledge base in serving as a bridge between the two cultures. Third, your starting point for hiring should probably be some aspect of human resources or personnel work, such as benefits administration, because these positions are often supplemented by other duties and responsibilities.

Some resources listing employers having this kind of position follow:

- *Directory of American Firms Operating in Foreign Countries.* Millis, MA: Uniworld Business Publications, 2005.
- *World Chamber of Commerce Directory* (chamberofcommerce.com).
- *Foreign Consular Offices in the United States* (Department of State, 2006) (state.gov/s/cpr/rls/fco). Lists addresses and phone numbers of consular officials who can advise you on American firms doing business in their countries.

International Not-for-Profit Organizations

Two good Internet sites to explore are International Jobs Center (international jobs.org) and InterAction (interaction.org). These both have excellent information about working for this kind of organization and allow you to review a sampling of job advertisements. Additionally, a keyword search on the Internet may yield you a variety of other websites to review.

Working Conditions

The six career paths outlined in this chapter share an appreciation for diversity, a curiosity about other cultures, and an interest in seeing diversity shared with others. Most of these positions also involve transitions and learning about change. Effective transitions require planning and an understanding of how people best accept change and how learning can be affected in a changing environment. These are also service jobs, and, like other careers in the helping professions, it can be difficult to define a typical day in any of them. When one is serving as a leader, teacher, helper, or guide, the need for change can come at different times. People in these positions must be comfortable with and flexible about their availability and accessibility.

It isn't just students who experience the transitions, either. Many administrators who have spent time shuttling between U.S. and foreign centers of operation will speak of their frustration in not having a home base and failing to fully develop relationships in either place because of this constant mobility. Others relish the constant change of scenery and their own ability to easily adapt to new locations, people, diet, and routine. Other work situations make some feel like travel agents who never get to take trips themselves—always advising people on destinations but never having the opportunity to go themselves. It's important in any job, and particularly in one that may involve residence in a foreign country, or even employment by a non-U.S. organization, to understand the nature of the job to be filled.

We can say these six different career paths share demands of accessibility, flexibility, planning, assistance, curiosity, and understanding. Each demands a unique approach to lifestyle, territoriality, need for personal space, and one's definition of "home."

American-Sponsored Private Schools Abroad

American-sponsored private schools abroad work very diligently not only to create communities for themselves, but also to create a community among all associated American schools around the world. In reading a publication such as *The International Educator* (tieonline.com), you become aware of the conferences, seminars, transfer assignments, field trips, and exchange programs that bring teachers and administrators of these schools into continual contact with one another. Many of these people obviously love international living and spend a few years at one school and move on to another interesting challenge. Solid work skills in budgetary matters, computer technology, and curriculum planning certainly are necessary, but the ability to make a home in many different places and to make friends and connections easily is also needed. The myth of private schools as having lower educational standards for their faculty and staff is quickly disabused as you read profiles of these professional educators. Educational standards are superb, and these private institutions seek out professional staff members who will enhance their reputations.

Foreign Study Exchange Programs

Foreign study exchange programs are administrative devices used to assemble and coordinate large numbers of exchanges through schools, language groups, and other organizations. Despite their apparent size as organizations, the staffs are in fact quite lean. Each individual tends to wear more than one organizational hat: record keeping, budgetary control, database development, marketing, and sales are some of the traditional tasks associated with working for these organizations. Staff members are frequently called on to travel and speak at schools and organizations about exchange program offerings. Though most are U.S. based, there may be opportunities to visit member institutions abroad or to lead tour groups to the host country.

American College Programs Abroad

American colleges maintaining campuses abroad and foreign schools offering special programs for American students often employ Americans to help staff these programs. Working conditions in these situations would be comparable to that of the staff of any college. Heavy involvement with students, considerable paperwork, and a fairly relaxed pace—except for traditionally busy times of the academic year—all characterize these positions. Certainly, living and working abroad would offer travel opportunities, language improvement, and the chance to meet and interact with foreign nationals on a daily basis.

Language skills would be put to a daily test in resolving student passport, visa, and work permit issues; negotiating living spaces for students; and helping with any contracts or lease arrangements. These skills would also be used in preparing guides for shopping, post office use, and transportation information as well as teaching orientation workshops for new arrivals.

International Student Programs

Student affairs staff members in this country who focus on international students are involved in much program planning and event production as well as a significant amount of counseling. They work with other departments of student affairs (health, career, physical education, college union, dining services) to integrate their international students into campus life while at the same time educating American students about their fellow students from other countries. Residential campus life positions include arranging and overseeing evening events and attending committee meetings to accomplish the student affairs mission.

Corporate Programs for Foreign Transfers

American corporate positions vary little whether they are located in the United States or overseas. Most corporations pride themselves on being able to prepare employees to take on their new settings and on accommodating employees' traditional American needs. Consequently, individuals working in human resources and hoping to serve as cultural liaisons will find the working conditions characteristic of any large corporation: fairly fast paced, exciting, competitive, well supplied with resources, and demanding of both qualitative and quantitative output measures for evaluation.

International Not-for-Profit Organizations

You will find most not-for-profit organizations characterized by a shared ideology that moves members toward a common goal. Organizations such as Food for the Hungry (fh.org), an evangelical Christian international relief organization; Save the Children (savethechildren.org); Christian Foundation for Children and Aging (cfcausa.org), a Catholic ecumenical worldwide charitable foundation; and World Vision (worldvision.org), a large Christian humanitarian organization, all have philosophies that underpin their efforts in the field. Because many of these organizations were built on an idea of change or political viewpoint, structure and organizational elements may be less than traditional. The flexibility may be freeing or it may be confining, depending on your personality.

Because many of these organizations operate on funding that is precarious, working conditions often mean physical settings that are less than ideal, lack of supplies, and the need to spend more time on development of funds than on the implementation of initiatives. But working for a nonprofit is often spiritually rewarding and may allow you to use your language skills on a daily basis.

Training and Qualifications

The discussion of career paths has made it clear that in each of these educational administration roles, the focus is not entirely on your language skills. Each employment environment will require different additional skills. If specific skills are not demanded, salary is apt to be quite low. These kinds of positions are perceived by many as very attractive, and supply far outweighs demand. Employers are aware of this and can be quite demanding of qualifications for positions that do not pay particularly well. Spend some time reviewing job postings in all areas of interest to become familiar with job requirements, pay scales for entry-level positions, and the associated lists of duties and responsibilities.

American-Sponsored Private Schools Abroad

Those interested in American schools abroad will find that most require U.S. certification and prefer teaching couples to single employees to help ensure an easy transition to being a minority in a foreign country. In addition, you

> **Director, International Education Institute.** A master's degree or equivalent training and in-depth knowledge of the U.S. educational system. At least seven years of administrative and supervisory experience in international education or a closely related field with some background in teaching or working abroad is required, as are strong analytical, budgeting, and interpersonal skills and the ability to organize a high volume of work effectively. Excellent writing and communications ability and demonstrated skill in preparing proposals, reports, and program materials are also desired.

may need coaching skills, curriculum planning, or other specialized administrative skills to win a spot in these kinds of organizations.

The following advertisement for an experienced director of an international study consortium for U.S. undergraduates seeking opportunities to study abroad is a good example of requirements. Entry-level positions would demand similar backgrounds, though fewer years of experience.

Foreign Study Exchange Programs

Working for a foreign study exchange program means understanding and having a background in both American and European schooling systems and having good budgetary and program leadership experience. Public presentation skills and some marketing and information publication design experience would also prove valuable. These organizations are in the business of recruiting students for a number of different programs. Because these programs may have high price tags, staff members must present a highly polished, professional image, master a wealth of detail, and be comfortable speaking in front of both small and large groups.

American College Programs Abroad

American colleges with programs in other countries will often hire administrators in the United States to work abroad administering programs on-site. A period of time on the American campus is critical to learn curricula, policies, and procedures and to ensure that the candidate can master the skills of the position. Student-advising experience with curriculums, some counseling, record keeping, and academic administrative experience will be looked at favorably as would your own previous participation in such a program and any periods of work, study, or travel abroad.

International Student Programs

The student affairs specialist may want to pursue further education in counseling or student affairs administration and take any steps possible while still in college to participate in the kinds of groups and activities he or she hopes to associate with as a professional. Any kind of event planning, budget responsibility, or leadership role and/or training would be helpful. These advisory positions require the use of counseling skills; knowledge acquired through either formal education or on-the-job training in volunteer positions will be looked at favorably. Production of information materials is a big part of these jobs, and experience in writing, editing, and publishing pamphlets is also helpful. As with all these types of positions, public presentation skills are crucial.

Corporate Programs for Foreign Transfers

Corporate liaison officers are often groomed for this position internally, and many already have established expertise in some aspect of human resources management. Areas of expertise might include, for example, benefits administration, outplacement, or retirement and life transitions counseling and referral. The liaisons' interest in and knowledge of the cultural environment they want to work in will also be important to the organization employing them. For example, if you have a Russian language background and have begun a career in human resources management, it would be important to alert your employer to your interest in a Russian posting when available. Once there, use your relocation to your best advantage, developing a good knowledge of the environs, shopping, theater, medical facilities, currency exchange, and perhaps produce a few fact sheets for use by your coworkers. If continued relocations of staff prove the need for a permanent corporate liaison official, you would then be well placed to apply.

International Not-for-Profit Organizations

The not-for-profit sector has become increasingly demanding of specialized talents among its workers and volunteers. Strong candidates may have skills in finance or accounting, agriculture or medicine, teaching or construction. Often, workers may need training in Teaching English as a Second Language (TESL). It is a mistake to believe that because these organizations are not-for-profit, their administration is less than excellent. In fact, to attract contributions, either personal or corporate, these organizations need to be highly organized and professional and display just the same competencies as their for-profit counterparts.

Another myth of the not-for-profit industry is that salaries are low. Low salaries exist, certainly, but there are also very competitive salaries today as not-for-profits realize that to gain and hold quality candidates they must pay comparable wages.

In Any Setting . . .

If you have elected to de-emphasize your language fluency or to use it as a secondary skill, then you must emphasize other talents that would make you employable. Even so, if you desire to stay in contact with the language you studied in college and have the opportunity to speak it, then when selecting educational administration positions, you would be well advised to carefully consider the career environments discussed in this chapter. Select the one most closely suited to what you have to offer or would be willing to add to your training and qualifications and then begin to take the steps necessary to match your experience more closely to job requirements for these positions.

Earnings

The six paths we have been discussing all involve the administration of programs that are international in scope and that will keep foreign language majors in touch with their language of study to some degree. They all emphasize valuing diversity, exploring unfamiliar cultures, and bringing enthusiasm and reassurance to others who may be less familiar with other cultures and consequently less accepting of them.

Your choice of a career path is an amalgam of many other smaller decisions and reflects your own value system. The business major who chooses corporate marketing certainly will realize a higher income than a marketing major who elects to use his or her skills in promoting AIDS awareness through public service videos for a nonprofit firm. Each has different values regarding income and work orientation.

For the foreign language major, too, different values make for different choices among these career paths based on length of workday, income level, relationships with coworkers, mobility, and stability. As we review some dimensions of each path, with a focus on earnings, consider carefully what you value, what you need, and what will make you happy. The earnings outlined for each path are generalizations only, gathered from numerous conversations with working professionals. Most of these employers are in the private sector, with the exception of state colleges and universities, and salaries are published only in the aggregate for a class of employees by title and years of experience. Compensation packages for positions abroad are completely individual, involving options such as flights home, housing, payment in U.S. dollars or the local currency, tuition assistance for dependents, movement of household goods, and countless site-specific perquisites that make comparisons meaningless.

American-Sponsored Private Schools Abroad

Negotiating salary packages is a crucial part of interviewing for an American private school position overseas. Packages can include spousal employment, tax incentives, and other add-ons that make comparisons between foreign postings very difficult. Websites such as The International Educator (tieonline.com), the official publication of the Overseas Schools Assistance Corporation, and NewsLinks, the publication of International Schools Services (iss.edu), have excellent information on salary and benefit negotiations. These reports will compare foreign teaching and administrative positions to their U.S. counterparts and try to make fair comparisons, even with all the nonsalary benefits. Entry-level salaries for administrators often start at around $27,000.

Foreign Study Exchange Programs

A foreign studies exchange program administrator could fill any number of roles: marketing, sales, recruitment, credentials processing, or direct-mail managing. Salaries would be competitive with other academic service enterprises. What may be disappointing about this type of position is your distance from the foreign community, unless you are afforded the opportunity to travel to member schools or lead groups of students on educational tours. These are consortium administration positions that are essential to bringing together and marketing large numbers of foreign study programs, but these positions might leave you feeling far away from the action and the use of your foreign language skills. The pay range here is quite broad, depending on the scope and size of the employer, with entry-level salaries from $26,000 to $34,000.

American College Programs Abroad

A job as an administrator for an American college at its non-U.S. campus will probably mean a salary based on a similar position in the United States, with adjustments made for the country in which you would be living. Whereas you might earn approximately $26,000 a year as an admissions representative for an American university in London, you might also be given a housing allowance or some cost-of-living adjustment for living in one of the most expensive cities in Europe. These positions begin at a level equivalent to $26,000 to $31,000 and up, depending on your experience.

International Student Programs

A student affairs specialist with a bachelor's degree working with international students would begin in the mid- to high-$20,000 range at most academic institutions and would have regular salary increases, opportunities for promotion, and, in most cases, a superior benefits package. Likewise, he or she might be able to take advantage of benefits offered by the academic employer to pursue an advanced degree at no or low cost to themselves.

Corporate Programs for Foreign Transfers

A corporate liaison for an international firm can earn a competitive corporate salary based on education and experience, with adjustments for foreign living.

These might include moving allowances, car maintenance costs, provision for children's schooling, housing allowance, cost-of-living allowance, and any number of salary adjustments based on the country. Promotions and increases would be similar to any competitive corporation, as would the effects of a competitive marketplace and the global economy on job stability.

There are two salary figures of importance here. An entry-level human resources officer position for a major corporation would begin at a salary of approximately $32,000. With the experience and seniority required to be competitive for an international posting involving corporate-liaison work for transferred employees, the salary would range from $50,000 to $68,000, depending on the associated benefits offered by the corporation to staff living abroad.

International Not-for-Profit Organizations
In many cases, fair or not, this type of not-for-profit employer assumes a psychic income based on working for the cause involved or in a foreign location. There may be no salary but, instead, a small stipend with housing may be provided. When there is a regular salary, it should come as no surprise that it is generally lower than comparable jobs in commerce and industry. More money is paid for unique skills, and many larger, established not-for-profit employers in the United States have competitive salary scales. Along with this has come an attendant bureaucratic complexity similar to any large organization and an increased competitiveness for jobs.

Review the salary information we have given you for American-sponsored private schools abroad, foreign study exchange programs, American college programs abroad, and international student programs, and know that if you decide to work for an international not-for-profit organization your salary will probably be lower than the other ranges we've shown. Some of the position titles generally open to entry-level workers include home-office manager, program manager, counselor, and outreach worker. Talk directly with a representative of the organization you are interested in to find out more about the entry-level salaries it offers or look to the websites we've posted previously to explore job listings and the salaries offered.

Career Outlook

You don't need to be a career specialist to notice the robust outlook for jobs in educational administration abroad. Talk to parents, neighbors, and classmates, and you will hear of family, friends, and friends of friends who are studying or living abroad or who have worked abroad for a period of time.

Notice the exchange students attending high school and colleges in this country and remember that they have their counterparts from your schools who are away in other countries learning equally valuable lessons about someone else's culture. The increasing ease of entering foreign countries and heightened interest in the exchange of ideas have made study, travel, and living abroad almost commonplace. Many schoolchildren, even at the elementary level, now have opportunities to begin their exploration of other lands at an age that whets their appetites for continued exploration later in life.

Through all these changes runs the theme of global interdependence for economic survival, peace, and control and eradication of disease, poverty, and hunger. The stewardship of the health of what we now perceive to be an increasingly fragile planet is also becoming more important. These global concerns have an impact on international programs because they alter the climate of exchange in a positive way and increase the willingness of countries to allow the movement of students and private citizens back and forth. This human exchange helps meet the needs of the planet's inhabitants. We now realize that our similarities far outweigh our differences.

The practical side of all of this is an increasing number of jobs for talented individuals with a background in a foreign language who want to use it to some extent in the administration of education programs. As with any growing sector of employment, popularity and growth bring change. The expected change here will be increasingly demanding criteria for employment as programs and the people who are to staff them become correspondingly sophisticated. That may mean employer demands for greater language skills, more extended travel and living abroad experience, and stronger skills packages in business, accounting, management, or administration to offer the employer other than foreign language as an auxiliary skill.

The current market for overseas study programs includes young people in increasing numbers whose parents have also experienced an educational program outside the United States. This adds to the level of expectation and demand for quality. Employers react by raising their eligibility standards for new hires in an effort to meet demands for better housing, more substantial course offerings, increased ease of transferring credits between institutions, and competitive fees for their programs. The lines of prospective job candidates get longer, but the number chosen does not rise in the same proportion.

The outlook is bright, the demands clear. Whether your focus is academic, nonprofit, or corporate, make sure that your language and cultural knowledge base is strong. Make every attempt to have some foreign travel and living abroad experience. A period of study in a formal curriculum program abroad is also highly advantageous. Most important, don't neglect developing a skills package. This may be fund-raising, benefits administration, program design and implementation, counseling and advising, or strong experience in organizing volunteers. You'll need some of each of these experiences and skills to enter and stay competitive in the field of educational administration for programs outside the United States.

Strategy for Finding the Jobs

The good news in the educational administration career path for foreign language graduates is the wide advertisement of these positions. All the possible employers we discuss in the career paths maintain high visibility to attract students, investors, and contributors. Many publish an array of attractive and informative literature detailing who they are and what their specific goals and objectives include. Your research in this area will go very quickly because of the high profile of all of these employers.

Learn All You Can

Acquire and read the literature you discover. Educational institutions have individual programs, a unique emphasis on student success or academic achievement, and various specific selling points they use to attract students. Not-for-profits are founded to support important ideas or positions on various issues, and you'll want to understand those. Corporations have products or services with individual features and selling points. It's important to learn about these and judge which setting may be most comfortable for you as a potential employee. We offer you here some excellent beginning resources to use in your search for employers. Left to your own devices, a visit to your college career office or exploring on the Internet will reveal many more.

Use Two Tactics

Locating the specific jobs can be approached on two fronts simultaneously. First, make sure you have access to the publications that advertise jobs in this area. We've listed some of these, such as *The International Educator* (tieonline.com), *Transitions Abroad* (transitionsabroad.com), and *The Chronicle of Higher Education* (http://chronicle.com). Keep a roster of who advertises the jobs you're seeking and put yourself on a regular schedule to check those advertisements and be ready to send a résumé and cover letter and any requested recommendations in response. This tactic is no different from other job searches. But these few publications do not cover the entire marketplace. Merely responding to their ads would not expose you to all the available jobs in educational administration that could be filled by a foreign language major.

Second, you'll need to take a more aggressive approach and initiate contact with some employers. Perhaps in your initial identification of employers, there were several institutional positions described that you haven't seen advertised. You may be hoping to administer the junior year abroad program on the French campus of an American college or perhaps you're seeking employment with a firm that packages study/travel/learn abroad programs for students. Maybe you'd like to put your administrative skills to use in a program providing medical doctors and materials to the African continent. You know these jobs exist, but they don't seem to appear in the want ads. To locate these employers, watch for advertisements of the programs being offered and then contact them to find out about employment possibilities.

Be Proactive, Not Reactive

You will need to reach out to these organizations, first by written correspondence, then by telephone, and finally, in person. Prepare a letter indicating your interest in the organization, your belief in how you could make a contribution, and some specifics on what form that contribution would take. How you express those thoughts will depend on both the thoroughness of your self-assessment and your appreciation for the mission and objectives of the organization, not to mention your persuasive ability.

Follow up your letter with a phone call to the individual you addressed in your letter. Try to arrange a mutually convenient time and place to sit down together and discuss your qualifications and the needs of the employer in greater detail. If distances are too great for a personal meeting, arrange a convenient time for a longer-than-usual phone conversation and prepare some good questions for your interview. Keep in mind, however, it's unlikely that one meeting will result in an offer of employment. If you develop some mutual interest, you might be invited to return for another meeting or be asked to pursue the relationship in another way, such as providing a writing sample or meeting a referral.

When an employer meets someone in this way who has obviously done his or her homework and made a concerted effort to understand the operation, it is difficult to dismiss the person, even if it is not a propitious time to hire. There may be an offer of part-time work leading to a full-time position. Or the employer might give you specific information about when an opening is expected to occur and encourage you to apply at that time, if you are still available. Occasionally, an employer will over hire in anticipation of a projected loss, rather than let a potentially valuable employee slip by.

Use What You Learn

No matter what kind of response you get, each of these experiences—letter writing, telephone calls, and visits—will only serve to sharpen your presentation skills, improve your ability to discuss aspects of your particular package of attributes, and help to increase your awareness about these employers' vocabulary, concerns, and issues. All of this information will further focus your ideas about where you can best fit in and what kind of job will make the best use of your talents.

Although you were probably aware of many of these occupational possibilities in college, they aren't necessarily environments you may know much about. As you talk to professionals in any of these areas, take brief notes to remind yourself of the issues and concerns that surface in your conversations. Read all you can find on international students here, Americans abroad, and exchange programs in general to begin to develop a stronger sense of the working life in the career paths. If you use the information you receive from your reading and contacts, you'll find that your conversations with potential employers become more informed. They'll see you as bright, aware, and on-target with their issues and therefore consider your candidacy seriously.

Professional Associations

Educational administration may seem very attractive to you, and there probably are several career paths that interest you, but you might find it bewildering to know where to actually begin. Begin with the people whose job it is to ensure the professional standards of their organizations, to promote the kind of work they do, and to interest others in it. Call or write them, and you will be amazed at the help they are willing to provide and the materials available.

Academic Travel Abroad
academic-travel.com

Association of American Schools in South America
aassa.com

China Educational Exchange
chinaeducationalexchange.org

Council on International Educational Exchange
ciee.org

Council on Standards for International Educational Travel
csiet.org

European Council of International Schools
ecis.org

Fulbright Program
http://exchanges.state.gov/education/fulbright

Institute of International Education
iie.org

International School Services
iss.edu

National Registration Center for Study Abroad
nrcsa.com

Office of Overseas Schools
state.gov/m/a/os

10

Path 5: Business, Industry, and Commerce

An international pharmaceutical company; the National Bank of Westminster, England; Starbucks; L.L. Bean; and Smith Barney: a seemingly disparate list, yet all these firms have something in common. They operate both in the United States and internationally. They conduct business with employees of many nationalities, in different political and economic environments, and in different time zones. The homogenizing effects of the computer screen, the telephone, and the fax machine cannot erase differences in culture. The umbrella of the same employer does not make every employee the same the world over. Differences remain that need to be understood, appreciated, and managed for success.

In a shrinking world economy, these multinational organizations need employees who can make a significant contribution to their firms in a specific department and also represent their companies outside of the United States with the respect and sensitivity expected of every company doing business in another culture. For example, the Japanese major who now does financial analysis for a firm in Tokyo knows that the Japanese character for the number four is pronounced the same as the word for death (*shi*). Consequently, some Japanese would not be enthusiastic about opening a new branch office on the fourth day of the month and yet may be reluctant to express that cultural bias to a foreigner for fear of seeming provincial or old-fashioned. In several countries, such as India, the use of the right and left hand are rigidly proscribed, and to contravene these cultural norms is to commit a gaffe. This is where your knowledge of a foreign language and culture will come in handy.

Definition of the Career Path

When seeking your first position in which foreign language talent is not the primary consideration, verify that the employer does offer some opportunity for using that skill. If, for example, you speak Russian and want to continue to be involved in that language and culture, beginning work in sales for a U.S. pharmaceutical company that has operations in Russia would be a good move. Your entry-level position would be as a pharmaceutical representative speaking to doctors about the clinical indications and situations best served by your line of prescription drugs. You'll receive sales training, develop product knowledge, and learn how to manage your own territory, schedule appointments, arrange out-of-town travel, and coordinate meetings with your district manager. Periodic sales conferences, refresher training, and home-office meetings will allow you to meet with other company executives who have contact with Russian operations and with whom you can discuss your interest. As you develop in your position and build a track record of success, you'll have an opportunity to apply for positions with your company's offices in Russia.

In fact, with increasing frequency, American businesses have been successfully launching branches in Russia. Fast-food operations such as Pizza Hut and McDonald's have captured the most media attention because they seem to represent ideological or cultural juxtapositions that Americans find interesting to read about or watch on the news. But these restaurant operations are just visible symptoms of a much larger effort by consumer goods retailers and manufacturers to find a market in the Russian Republic. When businesses do initiate plans to enter a new market such as Russia, one of the first things they do is to canvass their own employees to see who has knowledge of Russian language and culture, or travel experience, and what they might be able to offer in the planning process.

Many American software firms have found the Russian market particularly welcoming, because working with data and machine processes reduces some of the strains of communicating across cultural boundaries. Nevertheless, the American technician or consultant with a background in Russian language and culture would be a valuable member of a team sent overseas to sell a product, install it, or advise on its implementation. Computer science may be a language all its own, but in this case a little Russian on one side and some English on the other would work wonders.

Many foreign language majors working for firms with extensive dealings abroad never leave their desks in this country but instead "travel" all over the world every day via phone, fax, and e-mail to provide valuable services to clients and customers. Consider this job advertisement placed by a nonprofit international development and disaster relief agency:

Miami-based regional coordinator for Southern Africa: Needed to coordinate, administer, and communicate the agency's regional programs. Requires demonstrated involvement with grassroots development, relevant academic training or equivalent work experience, administrative abilities, and knowledge of Southern Africa.

The drop shipping of cargo (the movement of cargo contents from owner to owner on paper, even though the product itself may not physically leave the dock) often involves international communication. Financial brokerage houses do extensive business in currency buying and selling that involves international use of the telephone and fax machine.

Occasionally, a firm will reserve foreign service, especially in cities or countries deemed particularly desirable, as a reward for more senior staff. Regardless of your language or educational background, whether you've served with distinction, or whether you are interested in a period of foreign residency, some firms select staff to manage their foreign operations purely by seniority, assuming that these experienced individuals have the talent that is needed abroad. When you are interviewing with an organization that has international operations, even if your initial assignment is domestic, be certain to inquire how personnel for foreign posts are selected and whether such a post will ever be available to you as you grow in your career. Most firms will be quite candid with you during the interview about your chances of serving in a foreign branch office.

In the hospitality industry, a period of exposure to foreign life is considered essential to learning the traditions of fine dining, wines, and hotel management. A foreign assignment is often part of the younger employee's career training as he or she moves up the corporate ladder, perhaps on the way to becoming a chef, a hotel manager, or director of functions sales for a larger hotel where knowledge of the niceties of refined service are required to create a grand event or occasion. An individual might start with Holiday Inn in Cleveland as a functions sales manager, selling hotel services for weddings, sweet sixteen parties, summer corporate pool parties, and countless business functions, meetings, luncheons, and the like. These positions can be very creative: booking entertainment, providing decorations, assisting in food and beverage decisions, and helping to create the right ambiance and mood for an event. Successful progress in this area would lead to further advancement and might qualify you to spend time at a Holiday Inn abroad where you could be exposed to a more sophisticated menu, wine service, and guest amenities than are currently available in the United States. This kind of exposure to an older tradition of hotel-keeping helps to develop a level of service that will distinguish your work when you return to the United States.

American restaurant chains, pharmaceutical manufacturers, gun manufacturers, and even catalog operations such as L.L. Bean are expanding all across the globe. Staff in home-office positions frequently encounter regular mail, e-mail, telephone calls, and visits from representatives of these far-flung enterprises who will appreciate dealing with individuals who not only have some knowledge of their language but also sensitivity to their cultural context. This can be especially important in the Middle East, where behavioral norms and religious observances dictate work and social life to a far greater degree than is seen in the United States, and where Americans' likelihood of committing a social gaffe is greater without a cultural intermediary.

Advertising, banking, airlines, automobiles, architecture, and health services all present wonderful opportunities for work in other lands and for using other languages here in the United States. Even so, some additional cautions need to be delivered. In an era of instant communications, there is less need than ever before for extensive foreign staff. Video telephones, excellent air travel schedules, and automobile availability mean that frequent shorter visits, rather than extended stays in other countries, are more the norm.

Furthermore, as English continues to become the unofficial world language, residents of foreign countries whose English is excellent are often seen by U.S. firms as better choices for staff than Americans. Their salaries are frequently lower, they can be paid in the local currency, there is no hardship in their location, and they are fully conversant with the culture, language, and bureaucracy of the society. What's more, their English is often superb. Strong political and social pressure is often on the U.S. firm to hire local citizens. If there is resistance to the intrusion of a nonnative firm, it can be modified by the employment of resident workers. In increasing numbers of companies, through this combination of excellent transportation systems and telephone and fax communications, there is simply less need for a U.S.-staffed foreign branch or division of a firm.

Possible Job Titles

The following are possible job titles for positions that may use foreign languages as an auxiliary skill in business or commerce:

Market Analyst
Import/Export Coordinator/Expediter
Pharmaceutical Representative

Manufacturer's Representative
Program Director
In-Country Representative
Income Generation Specialist
Tour Director
Overseas English Language Media Staffer
Collaborative Projects Program Officer
International Banking Loan Officer
Management Consultant
Training and Development Specialist
Salesperson
Customer Service Manager

Possible Employers

You'll be pleasantly surprised at the range of firms that hire foreign language degree holders. Consider the following types of companies: environmental firms; sports organizations; advertising departments and agencies; banks, savings and loans, and credit unions; public relations departments and firms; software, hardware, and telecommunications manufacturers; hotels and motels; airlines, railroads, and cruise lines; hospitals and other health-care facilities; magazines, newspapers, radio stations, cable networks, and TV stations; professional associations; and manufacturing firms. Decide where you'd like to begin your search and use the resources listed at the end of this chapter and in the back of the book to help you locate that particular type of employer.

Working Conditions

We have suggested many possibilities for employment that do not revolve around your language fluency. This means that you will be using a unique combination of other skills and talents to attract an employer, not your language degree alone. As a foreign language major who has decided not to pursue language skill as the primary mechanism of employability, you are what the employer would term a generalist, or one who has varied or unspecified skills to bring to the organization.

We can make some predictions about your possible working conditions. Usually only larger organizations can afford to consider generalist candidates. Although a larger firm suggests a competitive salary and benefits package, it should also suggest many candidates vying for few places, so competition will be stiff. Because you may not have a specialized skill, there will probably be an initial training program, either a formal school for several weeks or an informal continuing program of training done during the week at scheduled times away from your regular duties. These training programs are designed not only to integrate you into the culture of your employer but also to help begin the process by which you build specific skills and knowledge the employer can draw on. In other words, without having majored in business, hotel and restaurant management, computer technology, or any other technical major, your principal task once you land a job will be to begin to develop some solid skills and experience in a specific area of business to remain attractive to your present and future employers.

You may not use your skills in a foreign language as your principal selling point in entering the job market. You may be hired partly for that skill and education but probably also because of your energy, enthusiasm, and potential to be molded to fit the needs of the organization. To grow within that organization or to move out of that organization, you will need to begin immediately to acquire more specific skills that will allow you to succeed on more concrete accomplishments than your original entry.

This initial training period bears little resemblance to the schooling you just completed. It is very demanding, your progress will be closely monitored, and you will be interacting with a number of company representatives who will, in most cases, meet to discuss your merits as an employee and to schedule assignments that make the best use of the attributes they perceive you to be demonstrating. It is a training period but a closely evaluated one.

Training and Qualifications

The training period that will make up the beginning of your employment will not only ensure your value to your current employer but also will build a foundation that will help to secure your continued worth in the workplace. Take full advantage of this entry training and of every possible training experience afforded you in your employment.

This training might be in an area such as financial analysis that captures your attention, and you might find you have an affinity for looking at quantitative data in a critical way. You will learn the various ways data can be interpreted for results and how to express those results to help management make effective decisions.

You might find you enjoy the area of human resources management and would like to learn more about the work classification system, drawing up job specifications, and determining duties and responsibilities and their associated pay levels. Or your interest might lie in benefits administration or cross training and staff development.

One area in which college seldom provides much exposure, even in the business major, is product management. This is the movement of a product from the raw material stage to the finished product, with countless opportunities for cost savings, efficiency modifications, and quality enhancement. It is an area of specialization all its own and attracts many talented people.

The principal reason for encouraging you to develop some particular skills is that in any job move after this first one, potential employers will be more critical of your past experience. As a new hire right out of college, most employers will give the nod to a four-year degree without expecting any specialized skills or knowledge. Your degree serves as a guarantee that you can learn what you need to know to become an effective employee. In this first hiring situation, some of your potential is taken on faith. It will not be this way again, so you must take advantage of your situation by becoming a skilled and knowledgeable employee.

Developing Specialized Skills

Let's say you are hired after college as a sales representative for a college textbook publisher. You learn your product line and do a good job of selling that product. You work independently out of your home with occasional supervisory visits and you make an excellent income. After five years, you tire of the routine of visiting college after college, and you decide to make a change. What skills other than college textbook selling have you acquired on the job in five years?

Interpersonal skills have been perfected and polished, certainly. But what about specific skills? A move to a different kind of job will be difficult, even more difficult than getting the first job out of college, because you now have five years of experience with one organization under your belt. But as far as qualifications go, what have you got to offer a new type of employer?

Now, what if during those five years, you asked your employer whether you could solicit some potentially publishable manuscripts from college faculty? Your request might be agreed to and some suggestions made about which fields might be most promising, perhaps the natural sciences. You solicit some materials or proposals for books, read them, make some suggestions and editorial comments, and forward them to your superiors for consideration. Perhaps one of these is published and you gain some recognition for skill and taste in selecting potential new authors and texts. This recognition could easily lead to a transfer to the home-office editorial department or new-product planning division, increasing your specialized skills and building valuable experiences for your résumé.

Maybe, in your first job, you have an opportunity to develop some plans and see them through to completion. Perhaps you can join a team whose main task is analysis and gain some particular familiarity with that work. You may be able to join a group doing marketing plans or fiscal planning or restructuring of staff. Additional computer training may be available as well as opportunities to attend evening graduate courses related to your work. Take advantage of all these opportunities, because they will help improve your next job presentation.

Not only will this initiative in seeking training improve your daily performance and help you to enjoy your job more, but it also will bring you the attention and possible promotions in status that are the rewards of exceptional effort. And if, like so many new employees, you decide after a year or two to refine your job prospects and seek other employment, your résumé will then display an entire new spectrum of skills that will make you attractive to another firm as a potential employee.

Additional Skills: Communication, Analysis, and Research

As a generalist with a liberal arts education, you bring to the workforce excellent oral and written communication skills. Much of your work in business organizations will revolve around communication: face-to-face, on paper, and electronic. Writing and using manuals, procedures, and memoranda, designing bulletin boards and electronic networks; and participating in meetings, meetings, and meetings will draw on your ability to communicate clearly, effectively, and powerfully. The following advertisement highlights the need for these skills:

Medical Staff Services Coordinator. Health-care services company seeks qualified individual to work in Physician Services Department. Individual will coordinate credentialing, licensing, and privileging of physicians, including day-to-day communications with various hospitals, interaction with billing and insurance companies, and verification of training and practice history. One to two years' health-care experience and/or B.A./B.S. degree in health care or business administration preferred. Seek highly organized, detail-oriented individual with excellent verbal and written communication skills. Must be able to work efficiently under tight deadlines and build effective relationships with regulatory boards and agencies. Competitive salary, excellent benefits, professional work environment.

Critical thinking is essential, too. Looking at problems and devising solutions will occupy much of your time. Expressing your ideas, interpreting situations, and determining patterns will challenge your ability to think creatively and systematically.

Perhaps you work for a public utility, and in analyzing your market research you notice an area with both a large percentage of Hispanic customers and a low number of requests for home service of gas appliances. Some investigation leads you to discover a lack of Spanish-speaking repair technicians and reluctance on the part of the Hispanic market to allow a repair person who speaks no Spanish into their homes. Introducing some Spanish-speaking repair technicians into this district is certain to be beneficial to both the customers and the utility.

Your research skills will allow you to compile and analyze relevant information and to present your findings so others can appreciate and use what you have discovered. You will be able to seek out helpful resources, formulate the relevant questions, and develop ways to supply and clarify the answers.

As a foreign language student, reading and memorization played a large part in your study habits. These are equally valuable skills to mention during an interview. The ability to amass and retain large amounts of detailed data will come in handy in the business world, as will your well-disciplined reading habits. There is always more than enough professional reading material to keep abreast of in business. Let your potential employer know that you are a reader and a learner.

Earnings

In this career path a variety of industries, employers, and job titles are discussed. To do justice to the corresponding variety of salaries possible for each would merit a volume of its own. Fortunately, if you have access to the Web (and don't forget your local library, which frequently will provide free Internet access to patrons for predetermined blocks of time), you can easily survey the salary surveys! The following are a few good starting places in your search for an estimated starting salary:

U.S. News and World Report Estimated Starting Salaries (usnews.com) is specifically designed for new college graduates and will feature thirty or forty academic majors and their starting salaries for the most recent year for which the survey has data (frequently that translates into two or three years previous to the current year). The *U.S. News and World Report* survey also indicates if the salaries have risen or fallen in the past year.

Another good site for wages and trends within employment areas is America's Career InfoNet, which can be found at acinet.org. This site takes a bit of getting used to, but once you learn how it operates, you can compare starting salaries in different geographic areas of the United States.

A very comprehensive salary website can be found on monster.com. This site is basically a list of links to many different salary and wage surveys. It includes familiar links, such as *U.S. News and World Report,* and specialized surveys for technical employment.

The government conducts ongoing salary and career surveys through the U.S. Department of Labor, Bureau of Labor Statistics (dol.gov or bls.gov). You can search for any number of jobs, read about what the work entails, about training and educational requirements, and about demand for the jobs, in addition to salary statistics.

Career Outlook

The career outlook for foreign language majors in business, industry, and commerce is excellent but highly competitive, with job growth better than average for managerial/executive, technical/engineering, media/advertising, travel/tourism, and banking/finance positions. The reasons are twofold. First, the employment candidate we have been discussing in this chapter is being hired for something in addition to his or her language skills: sales skill, financial acumen, managerial potential, or administrative abilities. Second, the involvement of businesses, even smaller firms, in international markets is growing rapidly. The projected strength of the European Community, increasing American investment in the Far East, and dramatic changes in the Russian economic structure all suggest possible new markets in the global economy.

Employers now and in the future will demand increasingly talented employees, and the individual who offers the unusual combination of foreign language talent and another useful skill will be seen as valuable. Today's most effective organizations involve their personnel in training and development. They cross train employees to learn about one another's duties and responsibilities. The staffing flexibility that results means the organization can respond more quickly to market demands, both the challenges and opportunities. The worker best poised for this situation is one with a well-rounded skills package.

Many foreign language majors employed in international business report that not until they went to work did they appreciate their education. They realized their degrees taught them far more than language skills. They learned about history, economics, politics, traditions, and personalities. In the work environment, this kind of information and the cultural nuances a foreign language major understands are seen as highly specialized and important knowledge.

The career outlook is clearly positive, but job seekers should be equally clear about what is required to participate in that future. You need a strong foreign language education, regardless of whether you intend to use it as a primary or an auxiliary skill. In the worlds of business, industry, and commerce you will need to have developed other skills to attract employers. Use your elective credits and your summers and vacations to build these skills packages. Most important, continue to learn all you can about the peoples, lands, and cultures that employ the language you have studied. You will then be able to seize any opportunity that might present itself in a volatile and multinational business environment.

Strategy for Finding the Jobs

Now that you have or will get a foreign language degree, you might be thinking, *Isn't the focus in international business on the business aspect of skills and not on the international?* Absolutely not! You have a job search advantage in this field that no other undergraduate degree, even business, can duplicate. As the world economy becomes increasingly global, even small and midsize firms are impacted in some way by international developments. You come to this job market with the undeniable proof that you've been thinking internationally for years: you have a degree in a foreign language.

Be Ready to Explain the Relevance of Your Degree

Now use this degree to your best advantage. The worlds of business, industry, and commerce have realized that no matter how much English dominates commercial transactions, it is critical to be able to reach out with the sensitivity and cultural awareness developed from studying the trading partner's language. There's no question that people like you are needed. You simply need to be ready to explain those strengths to an employer. Practice this by writing down how your foreign language studies can translate to the workplace environment you're interested in pursuing.

Find Out About Each Organization

The most appreciative audience for your credentials will be organizations currently doing business overseas or contemplating doing so. Without a business background, you will find that two strategies are critical. First, you need to know something about the organizations you will approach for employment. You might not be a trained accountant, marketer, or financial analyst, but you do have the intelligence and education to appreciate how an organization is structured, what its mission is, and what challenges and opportunities it currently faces.

Take the necessary steps to review some information on the organization. An annual report might not be as helpful in creating conversation in the interview as a recent newspaper or magazine article about the industry in general. Many organizations print brochures on opportunities for employment, their operating philosophy, their missions and goals, and any number of other topics. This material might be general, but it will convey the image and expectations of the organization. You can find this material in libraries, career offices, or simply by telephoning the organization and asking someone to send it to you. In addition, review the organization's website, which usually has valuable information about products, services, and mission statements.

Most employers are willing, and even expect, to do considerable on-the-job training once people are hired. To take the risk of hiring, they need to be assured that you have the flexibility, interest, and enthusiasm to learn all that's necessary. Your degree helps to reduce that risk. It proves you've already undergone some rigorous training in mastering your major. Your willingness to learn about the organization will go a long way in reassuring potential employers about your curiosity and interest in learning more.

The second strategy that you should employ if you lack a business background is outlined in the next section.

Relate Your Skills and Abilities to the Business Employer's Needs

You must help the employer understand how you see yourself contributing to the organization. As they read your résumé, you don't want them to think, *Does this person want to be posted overseas?* or *This person is an interpreter; how will I use him or her?* Let the employer know up front that, although you do have language training and you hope to put it to good use for the organization someday, your first goal is to learn the ropes and to build an expertise for yourself that the organization can utilize.

Once a mutual understanding of both your abilities and the organization's needs has been reached, be ready to speak specifically and concretely about the skills and attributes you have identified through your self-assessment and the experiences documented on your résumé. Build a strong skills package statement for yourself, to which the employer will respond, "Yes, I need that!"

Highlight Specific Skills

In your contacts with employers, especially during interviews, learn how to focus attention on what you do well. You're a foreign language major, not a business major, so focus interview attention on your unique and valuable skills and knowledge base. Rather than discussing accounting procedures, you might talk about the effects of the European Community on national pride. Take stock of your special abilities and keep the interview focused on what you know and do well. This might include reading, writing, and speaking skills; problem analysis; and critical thinking. You might also have some specialized awareness of social customs or political systems or have done an in-depth study on some aspect of a culture. Business is part of the social fabric of a society, and any new business, especially one from another country, will try very hard to integrate itself into the new culture. You can play a vital role in that integration process.

Stay Current

As you read about and research the companies you are contacting, try to relate what you learn about their current status, problems, and recent successes to what you have to offer in your skills package. Once you have established a track record and created a definable niche in the organization, then, if the need arises, you can begin exploring how to use your foreign language skills more directly with that employer.

Professional Associations

A wide range of types of employers have been described, and a correspondingly wide range of professional associations is provided here. Examine the list to see which groups you might want to contact to get additional information about career choices, job opportunities, or professional development assistance.

Alliance for Nonprofit Management
allianceonline.org

American Association of Advertising Agencies
aaaa.org

American Association for Physical Activity and Recreation
aahperd.org/aapar

American Bankers Association
aba.com

American Health Care Association
ahca.org

American Hospital Association
aha.org

ASD Cultural Exchange
http://asdculturalexchange.com

Hospitality Sales and Marketing Association International
hsmai.org

Magazine Publishers of America
magazine.org

National Association of Broadcasters
nab.org

National Association of Environmental Professionals
naep.org

National Association of Manufacturers
nam.org

National Newspaper Association
nna.org

National Sporting Goods Association
nsga.org

Public Relations Society of America
prsa.org

Software and Information Industry Association
siia.net

Telecommunications Industry Association
tiaonline.org

Travel Industry Association of America
tia.org

Additional Resources

Academic Employment Network
266 Gray Rd.
Windham, ME 04062
academploy.com

American Association of University Professors
1012 Fourteenth St. NW, suite #500
Washington, DC 20005
aaup.org

American Bank Directory
http://american-bank.addresses.com

American College Testing
Educational Services Division
500 ACT Dr.
P.O. Box 168
Iowa City, IA 52243
act.org

American Federation of Teachers
555 New Jersey Ave. NW
Washington, DC 20001
aft.org

American Institute for Foreign Study
River Plaza

9 West Broad St.
Stamford, CT, 06902
aifs.com

America's Career InfoNet
acinet.org

America's Job Bank
ajb.dni.us

America's Top Medical, Education, and Human Services Jobs
JIST Works, Inc.
8902 Otis Ave.
Indianapolis, IN 46216
jist.com

Best's Insurance Reports
A.M. Best Co.
Ambest Rd.
Oldwick, NJ 08858
ambest.com

The Boston Globe
The Globe Newspaper Co.
135 Morrissey Blvd.
Boston, MA 02107
boston.com

CareerBuilder
careerbuilder.com

The Career Guide: Dun's Employment Opportunities Directory
Dun & Bradstreet Corporation
103 JFK Pkwy.
Short Hills, NJ 07078
dnb.com

Catholic Almanac
Our Sunday Visitor, Publishing Division
200 Noll Plaza

Huntington, IN 46750
osv.com

The Chronicle of Higher Education
1255 23rd St. NW
Washington, DC 20037
http://chronicle.com

The College Board Guide to Jobs and Career Planning
by Joyce Mitchell
The College Board
45 Columbus Ave.
New York, NY 10023
collegeboard.org/index.html

College Grad
collegegrad.com

College Placement Council Annuals
62 Highland Ave.
Bethlehem, PA 18017
naceweb.org

The Complete Guide to Public Employment
by Ronald Krannich and Caryl Krannich
Impact Publications
9104 Manassas Dr., suite N
Manassas Park, VA 20111-5211
impactpublications.com

The Complete Mental Health Directory
Grey House Publishing
185 Millerton Rd.
P.O. Box 860
Millerton, NY 12546
greyhouse.com

Council on International Educational Exchange
7 Custom House St., 3rd floor
Portland, ME 04101
ciee.org

Dictionary of Occupational Titles
U.S. Department of Labor
http://stats.bls.gov

Directory of Adventure Alternatives in Corrections Mental Health and Special Populations
Association of Experiential Education
3775 Iris Ave., suite #4
Boulder, CO 80301
aee.org

Directory of American Firms Operating in Foreign Countries
Uniworld Business Publications
3 Clark Rd.
Millis, MA 02054
uniworldbp.com

Encyclopedia of Associations
Thomson Gale
27500 Drake Rd.
Farmington Hills, MI 48331
gale.com

ERIC Clearinghouse on Languages and Linguistics
cal.org/ericcll

Experiment in International Living
1 Kipling Rd.
Brattleboro, VT 05301
usexperiment.org

Federal Jobs Digest
Breakthrough Publications
326 Main St.
Emmaus, PA 18049
jobsfed.com

Foundation Grants to Individuals
The Foundation Center
79 Fifth Ave.

New York, NY 10003
fdncenter.org

Graduate Management Admission Test
Graduate Management Admission Council
1600 Tysons Blvd., suite #1400
McLean, VA 22102
gmat.org

Graduate Records Exam
Graduate Records Examination Board
Educational Testing Services
P.O. Box 6000
Princeton, NJ 08541
gre.org

Harrington-O'Shea's Career Decision-Making System
American Guidance Service
5601 Green Valley Dr.
Bloomington, MN 55437
agsnet.com

Harvard University Gazette
Harvard Office of News & Public Affairs
Holyoke Center 1060
Cambridge, MA 02138
hno.harvard.edu/gazette

The Helping Professions: A Careers Sourcebook
by William R. Burger and Merrill Youkeles
Thompson/Wadsworth
thomsonedu.com

Hoover's Handbook of American Business
Hoover's, Inc.
5800 Airport Blvd.
Austin, TX 78752
hoovers.com

Hospitals Directory
healthcarehiring.com

Hot Jobs
hotjobs.com

Human Service Career Network
P.O. Box 399
Sullivan, MO 63080
hscareers.com

Index of Majors and Graduate Degrees
College Board Headquarters
45 Columbus Ave.
New York, NY 10023
http://store.collegeboard.com

Internships 2006
Peterson's Guides series
Thomson/Peterson's
Princeton Pike Corporate Center
2000 Lenox Dr.
P.O. Box 67005
petersons.com

Job Bank Series:
Atlanta Job Bank
Boston Job Bank
Chicago Job Bank
Dallas/Ft. Worth Job Bank
Denver Job Bank
Detroit Job Bank
Florida Job Bank
Houston Job Bank
Los Angeles Job Bank
Minneapolis Job Bank
New York Job Bank
Ohio Job Bank
Philadelphia Job Bank
San Francisco Job Bank
Seattle Job Bank
Washington, D.C. Job Bank
F+W Publications Inc.
4700 E. Galbraith Rd.

Cincinnati, OH 45236
adamsmedia.com

Job Finders Online
Planning/Communications
7215 Oak Ave.
River Forest, IL 60305
planningcommunications.com/jf/index

JobHunt
job-hunt.org

JobWeb.com
jobweb.com

Medical and Health Information Directory
Thomson Gale
Inbound Sales
27500 Drake Rd.
Farmington Hills, MI 48331
gale.com

Million Dollar Directory: America's Leading Public and Private Companies
The D&B Corporation
103 JFK Pkwy.
Short Hills, NJ 07078
dnbmdd.com/mddi

Modern Language Association
mla.org

Monster Jobs
monster.com

Moody's Manuals
Moody's Investors Service
Moody's Corporation
99 Church St.
New York, NY 10007
moodys.com

Myers-Briggs Type Indicator
Consulting Psychologists Press, Inc.
1055 Joaquin Rd., 2nd floor
Mountain View, CA 94043
cpp-db.com

National Education Association
1201 16th St. NW
Washington, DC 20036-3290
nea.org

National Job Bank
nationaljobbank.com

National Trade and Professional Associations of the United States
Columbia Books Inc.
P.O. Box 251
Annapolis Junction, MD 20701
columbiabooks.com

Occupational Outlook Handbook
Occupational Outlook Quarterly
U.S. Department of Labor
Frances Perkins Building
200 Constitution Ave. NW
Washington, DC 20210
dol.gov

O'Dwyer's Directory of Public Relations Firms
J.R. O'Dwyer Co. Inc.
271 Madison Ave.
New York, NY 10016
odwyerpr.com

Peterson's Graduate Schools in the U.S.
Thomson/Peterson's
Princeton Pike Corporate Center
2000 Lenox Dr.
P.O. Box 67005
petersons.com

Preparing Future Faculty
preparing-faculty.org

Sports Marketplace Directory
Grey House Publishing
P.O. Box 860
185 Millerton Rd.
Millerton, NY 12546
sportsmarketplace.com

Standard and Poor's Register of Corporations, Directors & Executives
Standard and Poor's Corporation
55 Water St.
New York, NY 10041
standardandpoors.com

Strong Interest Inventory
Consulting Psychologists Press, Inc.
1055 Joaquin Rd., 2nd floor
Mountain View, CA 94043
cpp-db.com

United Nations
un.org

World Wide Chamber of Commerce Guide
chamberfind.com

World Wide Worker
worldwideworker.com

Index